EVER WONDER
HOW MUCH YOU KNOW?

1. Why is a wedding ring always worn on the third finger?
   a. It was once thought to be the site of the vein of love.
   b. It is the least-used finger of the five.
   c. It is the easiest to measure for a fitting.

2. What is the origin of the phrase "son of a gun?"
   a. The male children of gunslingers in the Old West.
   b. Sons conceived on board a ship, where a secret rendezvous often took place near the midship gun.
   c. Illegitimate children sired by soldiers during foreign wars.

3. Why do bats sleep upside down?
   a. So blood will rush to their heads, helping them to see in the dark.
   b. Heat rises, and that's how they keep warm.
   c. So they can hang from the cave ceiling and avoid predators.

ANSWERS 1) a;   2) b;   3) c.

EVER WONDER WHY?

Douglas B. Smith

FAWCETT

BALLANTINE BOOKS · NEW YORK

A Fawcett Book
Published by The Random House Publishing Group
Copyright © 1991 by Douglas B. Smith

Published in the United States by Fawcett Books, an imprint of The Random House Publishing Group, a division of Random House, Inc., New York.

Fawcett is a registered trademark and the Fawcett colophon is a trademark of Random House, Inc.

www.ballantinebooks.com

Library of Congress Catalog Card Number: 91-92209

ISBN 0-449-14746-0

Manufactured in the United States of America

First Edition: January 1992

OPM 29 28

To Jeannette and David

Acknowledgments

The author gratefully acknowledges the invaluable assistance received from James Ellisor, Knox Burger, Lorene Arledge, Dr. O. F. Schuette of the University of South Carolina Department of Physics, the research staff at the South Carolina State Library in Columbia, and the many experts and specialists who provided information. Thanks is also given to the many people who provided the author with challenging and intriguing questions, with particular thanks going to Lottie McMahon and Brent Smith.

Preface

Ever wonder why books have prefaces?

The word *preface* comes from a Latin word *praefatio*, which means "to speak before." The purpose of a preface, then, is to speak to the readers before they read the main part of the book and tell them what the book is about.

This is a book about WHY: why so many barns are red, why Southern men are nicknamed "Bubba," why you never see cashew nuts in their shells, why breaking a mirror is seven years bad luck, why a square boxing enclosure is called a "ring," and why you see those crescent moons carved into outhouses. If questions like these make you wonder, you will like this book. It answers about three hundred such questions, with the emphasis in every case being on *why* something is the way it is. Not who, what, when, where, or how, but why. "Why?" is the first question we learn to ask as children and the one our parents have the hardest time answering. This is because "Why?" is the most difficult question to research. Books and other publications answer lots of questions about their subjects, but for some reason not usually questions about why. A book on barns may not tell you why so many of them are red, a book on cats might not reveal why their eyes glow in the dark, and a book on marriage customs might not say why the bride stands on the groom's left. Because of this, 'why' questions usually require a lot of digging in strange places. While it is true that some answers can be found rather quickly in obvious places like encyclopedias or other standard reference sources, more often they require research in obscure books, old periodicals, government documents, business publications, trade journals, and frequently consultation with one or more experts. Finding an acceptable answer can take days, months, or longer. For instance, the author has spent over two years trying to find an answer to the question of why yawns are contagious. So far, no luck.

On the other hand, there are times when too many answers can be found. That is, research turns up conflicting explanations from two or more seemingly unimpeachable sources. When this happens, the explanation about which there seems to be the greatest degree of consensus is the one used in this book. In the absence of such a consensus, the explanation that seems most plausible is the one used.

About half of the questions in this book were submitted by other people; the other half are questions that have intrigued —and sometimes plagued—the author during the past thirty years.

It has been the author's experience that almost everyone has a deep curiosity about the underlying reasons for the things they see about them. It was with this in mind that this book was written.

Ever Wonder Why?

—when a lady spurns a gentleman, she is said to be "giving him the cold shoulder"?

Despite current usage, the phrase does not have a romantic origin. In fact, the shoulder in "cold shoulder" is actually a shoulder of mutton!

In the early nineteenth century, when the phrase was first recorded by Sir Walter Scott, it was customary for a hostess to serve hot meat to visitors who were welcomed and cold meat to those who had overstayed their welcome. Since the cold meat given to the unwanted guest was usually a shoulder of mutton, the hostess was said to be "giving him the cold shoulder"—of mutton, that is.

—he-men sailors of old often wore earrings?

In the days of the wooden sailing ship, there was no certainty that sailors setting out on a long voyage would ever see their homeland again. To prepare for the worst, sailors took to wearing gold earrings so that if there was an accident and their bodies were found washed ashore on some foreign beach, the gold in the earrings would be used to pay for decent burials.

—red is the traditional color for barns?

Late in the 1700s, American farmers began painting their barns with homemade wood preservatives to protect them from the weather. In the northern states where winters are particularly harsh, the preservative found to offer the best protection was one made from lime, skim milk, and red iron oxide. When this mixture dried, it gave the barn a durable, plasticlike finish. Because of the iron oxide, it also gave the barn a bright red color. The use of this preservative became so widespread that by the early 1800s red had become the traditional color for barns.

1

Ever Wonder Why?

—dimes, quarters, and half-dollars have notched edges, while pennies and nickels do not?

The U.S. Mint began putting notches on the edges of coins containing gold and silver to discourage holders of such coins from shaving off small quantities of the precious metals. Before coins were notched, shaving was a common practice, and at one point the problem was so bad that merchants refused to accept coins without first weighing them to determine their true value. Notching the coins corrected the problem since any attempt to shave a notched coin could be easily detected.

Dimes, quarters, and half-dollars are notched because they contain silver. There is no need to notch pennies and nickels since the metals they contain are not valuable enough to make shaving worth the effort.

—corned beef is called corned beef when it contains no corn?

The "corned" in corned beef has nothing to do with the vegetable corn. It means "preserved in salt." The salt pellets originally used to preserve this type of beef were called salt "corns," and beef preserved in this way was called corned beef.

Ever Wonder Why?

—riders always mount their horses from the left?

The custom began centuries ago when men carried swords. Since most men are right-handed, the sword was usually carried on the left hip to make it more accessible to the right hand. With a long sword dangling from a rider's left side, it was clearly easier for him to mount his horse by putting his left foot into the stirrup and then throwing his right leg across the horse's back. This, of course, required that the horse be mounted from the left. Even after riders no longer carried swords, mounting from the left remained the custom.

—zero scores in tennis are called "love"?

In France, where tennis first became popular, a big, round zero on the tennis scoreboard looked like an egg and was, in fact, called an egg, which in French is *l'oeuf*. When tennis became popular in this country, Americans copied the French and also called the zero score *l'oeuf* but pronounced it "love."

—the symbol for a pawnshop is three golden balls?

The three golden balls were originally the symbol of the Medici family of Florence, who were the owners of many pawnshops in Italy during the Middle Ages.

According to legend, Averado de Medici, while serving under Charlemagne, once slew a giant warrior named Mugello on whose mace were three golden balls. To commemorate his victory, Averado adopted these balls as a device on the Medici family coat of arms. Later, the balls were displayed over the entrances of the de Medici pawnshops and eventually came to symbolize pawnshops in general.

3

Ever Wonder Why?

—someone suspected of expressing an insincere emotion is said to be shedding crocodile tears?

This expression arises from the fact that crocodiles often appear to shed tears, but not for emotional reasons. When a crocodile takes a big bite of something, the food presses against the top of its mouth, causing a watery liquid to ooze from its eyes. These apparent tears aren't, of course, genuine, and the crocodile is still the same dangerous reptile ready to attack anything that comes within its reach. Hence the expression.

—English pubs have strange names like The Lamb and Circle, The Golden Dove, and The Sword and Plume?

Before reading became a basic skill, merchants found it necessary to identify their shops with objects or pictures. Barbers used a red and white pole, pawnbrokers used three golden balls, and shoemakers used a picture of a shoe. This enabled customers who couldn't read to find the shops they were seeking.

When it came to identifying the many pubs in England, the owners found that there was no way to draw pictures illustrating Adam's Pub, McDuffy's Tavern, etc. So they gave their pubs names that could be pictured—names like The Lamb and Circle and The Golden Dove.

—the color black is used for mourning?

Because our ancestors were afraid of ghosts!

Our ancient forebears believed that ghosts would be lurking about at the site of a recent burial looking for a living body to invade. They tried to hide from the ghosts by painting their white skins black. Later, black clothes were used for the same purpose.

Ever Wonder Why?

—a hamburger is called a hamburger when it contains no ham?

The Tartars, a Turkic-speaking people who lived in central Asia, were rugged, nomadic horsepeople who ate raw beef. Rugged though they were, they soon decided that raw meat would be a lot easier to chew if they could find a way to tenderize it. Eventually, they did find a way. Before a long day's ride, they would put a slab of beef under their saddles and let the up-and-down motion of the horse pound the meat to bits. At the end of the ride they would scrape the tender morsels into a heap, season it with salt, pepper, and onion juice, and eat what today we call steak tartare.

A merchant from Hamburg, Germany, who was doing some trading in Asia in the mid-nineteenth century, came upon the Tartars' recipe and took it back to Germany, where it was introduced as Hamburg steak. Later, a cook in Hamburg decided to broil the meat, and by the end of the nineteenth century this concoction was called hamburger meat.

Hamburger meat, it is believed, was brought to the United States in the 1800s by German immigrants. In 1904, at the World's Fair in St. Louis, broiled hamburger patties in buns were sold for the first time and called just "hamburgers."

—cash registers ring?

A cash register rings to announce that someone has opened the cash drawer and has access to the cash. It was hoped that, by drawing attention to the opening of the cash drawer, the bell would discourage employee theft. In fact, one of the first cash registers with a bell was called a "thief catcher."

Ever Wonder Why?

**—men's clothes have buttons on the right
and women's clothes have buttons on the left?**

It is easier for right-handed people to push buttons on the right through holes on the left, and since most people are right-handed, this is why men's clothes have buttons on the right. But what about women, who are also mostly right-handed?

When buttons first came into being, they were very expensive and were worn primarily by the well-to-do. Women in that class did not usually dress themselves but were dressed by maids. Since a maid would be facing a woman she was dressing, dressmakers put the buttons on the *maid's* right, and this, of course, put them on the woman's left where they have remained.

**—it is an expression of contempt to say
someone's name is "mud"?**

John Wilkes Booth, the man who assassinated Abraham Lincoln, fractured his leg while escaping from Ford's Theater. A country doctor who knew nothing of the assassination treated Booth and sent him on his way. Later, when the doctor realized whose leg he had treated, he notified the authorities and as a result was imprisoned as a co-conspirator. Later, the injustice was recognized, and he was pardoned by President Andrew Johnson.

The doctor's name was Samuel Mudd, and soon after the assassination it became an expression of contempt to say that someone's name was "Mudd." Over time, people forgot the origin of the expression and "Mudd" became "mud."

Ever Wonder Why?

—dogs sometimes turn around several times before they lie down for a nap?

Domestic dogs, being descendants of wild dogs, still retain some of the wild dog's natural instincts. One of these instincts, it is believed, accounts for the way dogs often prepare for a nap.

Since wild dogs live in the forest or the brush, they often have had to trample down grass and weeds to make a comfortable place to lie down. They do this by walking around and around in a tight circle. It is speculated that remnants of this instinct may account for the domestic dog's tendency to turn around a few times before it lies down for a nap.

—so many umbrellas are black?

When umbrellas first came into wide use during the 1700s, they were made of oil-soaked cotton cloth stretched over whalebone. The purpose of the oil was to make the cotton cloth waterproof, but it also gave the cloth a blackish color.

This type of umbrella was, in fact, very waterproof but not very durable. Soon, newer and better umbrellas were developed, and since the color black had come to be associated with effective waterproofing, most of the newer models were dyed black.

Ever Wonder Why?

——someone who bears the blame for the mistakes of others is called a "scapegoat"?

The origin of this expression is found in the Bible. In Leviticus, chapter XVI, the ritual to be performed on the Annual Day of Atonement is described as follows:

> And Aaron shall lay both his hands upon the head of the live goat and confess over him all the iniquities of the children of Israel, and all their transgressions, even all their sins. And he shall put them upon the head of the goat and shall send him away by the hand of an appointed man into the desert. And the goat shall bear upon him all their iniquities. And he shall let the goat escape into the wilderness . . .

This goat, bearing on its head all of the sins of the children of Israel, came to be referred to as the "escaping goat" and later as just the "scapegoat." This led to the term being applied to a person made to bear the blame for others.

Ever Wonder Why?

—geese fly in V formation?

Any statement about why animals do what they do is, of course, arguable, and in this case there appear to be two theories about why geese fly in a V formation.

The first holds that the V formation allows each bird to take maximum advantage of disturbances in the air created by the flap of the bird in front. Such disturbances tend to be generated in an inverted V pattern very similar to the formation flown by the geese.

The second theory states that, because the bird's eyes are located on the sides of its head, the V formation provides each bird with the best simultaneous view of the flock leader and the direction of the flight.

Readers can decide for themselves which theory seems most plausible. Perhaps the real reason is a combination of both theories. Only the geese know for sure.

—the color blue is used for baby boys?

Centuries ago, it was commonly believed that satanic spirits hovered about nurseries waiting for a chance to enter the bodies of young children. It was also believed that these evil spirits could be repelled by the color blue, the color of the heavens. Even today, in the Mideast, certain Arabs still paint their doorways blue to keep away evil demons.

Since it was felt to be of crucial importance to protect young males, it became the custom to dress them in blue to ward off any evil spirits that might be lurking about.

Much later, so that baby girls would also have a color, it was decided to assign to them pink, the color of the rose.

Ever Wonder Why?

—Canadians say "mush" to make their
sled dogs move?

The Canadian sled drivers are actually trying to say "marchons," which means "let us march" in French. The early French-Canadians used this command to make their sled dogs go forward. When English-speaking drivers tried to copy the expression, they mispronounced it "mushon" and later abbreviated it to just "mush."

—circus acts are performed in rings?

The modern circus was first conceived in 1763 by an ex-cavalry officer named Philip Astley, and the main attraction in Astley's circus was trick riding on horseback. Astley discovered very quickly that his riders could stay on their horses with much greater ease when the horses were made to gallop in a tight circle. To guide the horses in these circles, Astley placed round structures—or rings—on the circus floor, where they remained during the entire circus performance.

It was another circus owner, Antonio Franconi, who determined that the optimum diameter of the circus ring was 42 feet, the size used today.

It is interesting to note that the word *circus* comes from the Latin word for circle.

Ever Wonder Why?

—so many coin banks are shaped like pigs?

Long ago, dishes and cookware in Europe were made of a dense, orange clay called "pygg." When housewives began saving coins in jars made of this clay, the jars became known as "pygg banks." In the nineteenth century, an English potter misunderstood the meaning of the old term "pygg" and took it to mean "pig." So when someone asked him to make a pygg bank, he made one shaped like a pig. The idea caught on, and soon everyone wanted a "piggy" bank.

—a woman who pays her own way on a date is said to be "going Dutch"?

This expression originated in the seventeenth century when the Dutch and English were both business and military rivals. During that period the English held the Dutch in very low esteem, and this was reflected in many of their expressions. A "Dutch bargain" was a one-sided deal, "Dutch courage" was courage gotten from a bottle, and a "Dutch nightingale" was a frog. So, if a man asked a woman out and then let her pay her own way, the woman was said to be receiving a "Dutch treat," and the couple was said to be "going Dutch."

—a quarter is called "two bits"?

The "bits" referred to are actually bits, or pieces, of a Spanish coin that was popular in eighteenth-century America. The coin, the Spanish dollar, was made of silver and was so large that it was often cut into eight smaller parts, each worth $\frac{1}{8}$ of a dollar or 12½¢. Thus, when the American quarter came into use, it was said to be worth "two bits."

Ever Wonder Why?

—people shake hands to show friendship?

In very early times, most men carried weapons and wielded them in their right hands. When a man wanted to show another that he wished to be friendly, he extended an empty right hand showing that it contained no weapon. Then, to make absolutely sure that neither man could suddenly reach for a weapon, each man grasped the hand of the other and held it firmly until each was sure he was dealing with a friend. The actual shaking of the hand may have been for the purpose of dislodging any weapons hidden in sleeves.

—the eyes in a portrait seem to follow you around the room?

You know an eye is looking at you when you see the very front of the eye; you know it is looking away from you when you see a side view of the eye.

If an artist paints the front view of an eye, then that is the only view there is. Since the painting is a flat surface, one cannot walk around and get a side view of the eye. One can see only the front view the artist painted, and that is why the eyes seem to follow you around the room.

Ever Wonder Why?

—the press is called the "fourth estate"?

In the days of feudalism the word *estate* meant any of three social classes having a great influence on political affairs. These classes were the church, the nobility, and the common people. In England around the nineteenth century, it became apparent that there was another estate also exercising influence over public affairs, that estate being the press. In 1828 Thomas Macaulay—referring to the reporters' gallery in Parliament—wrote in the *Edinburg Review*, "The gallery in which the reporters sit has become a fourth estate of the realm." Thus began the practice of referring to the press as the fourth estate.

Ever Wonder Why?

—black cats are thought to be unlucky?

During the Middle Ages, parts of Europe were overrun with cats, many of which were adopted as pets by the poor. When witch hysteria hit Europe in the sixteenth century, many poor old women of the streets were accused of being witches and their cats of being their evil accomplices. Hence, cats—once revered as sacred in some countries—were now thought to be evil.

The black cat may have gotten its particular reputation as a result of a story told in England in the 1560s. As the story goes, a father and son were walking along a dark road in Lincolnshire one night when they were frightened by a small, dark creature running across their path. They pelted the creature with stones and watched it limp away to a nearby shack known to be the home of an old woman suspected of being a witch. By the light of a window the father and son saw that the small creature was, in fact, a black cat. The next day, the old woman appeared in town with a bruised face, bandaged arm, and a limp. This led the townspeople to conclude that the black cat had actually been the old woman, transformed, out for a nightly prowl. Thereafter, all of the woes that befell the father and son were said to be a direct result of the witch crossing their path on that dark night in the form of a black cat. This led people to suspect all black cats of being some form of evil in disguise and of being bearers of extremely bad luck.

—a jeep is called a "jeep"?

When this vehicle, a quarter-ton reconnaissance car, was first delivered to the army, it was called a "general purpose" vehicle and had the letters "GP" painted on its side. This led to the vehicle's being called a "jeepee" and then a "jeep."

Ever Wonder Why?

—the mile is exactly 5,280 feet?

In ancient Rome land distances were measured in paces, one pace being defined as two steps, or about 5 feet. The largest unit of land measure used by the Romans was the *milia passuum*, which is Latin for "a thousand paces." Since one pace was equated with 5 feet, a *milia passuum* was 5,000 feet.

Great Britain, once a part of the Roman Empire, adopted the *milia passum* but abbreviated it to "mile." Now the British also used another unit of land measure called the furlong, which was defined as 660 feet, the approximate length of a plowed furrow in an ordinary field. (The word *furlong* is actually a contraction of "furrow long.") The furlong was used extensively in surveying, and when it became apparent that the mile would also be used in surveying, it was decided that the mile should be a whole number of furlongs. Since the mile was 5,000 feet and the furlong was 660 feet, it was decided to change the mile to exactly 8 furlongs, or 5,280 feet. In 1575 Elizabeth I passed a law equating the mile to exactly this number.

Ever Wonder Why?

—descendants of nobility are called "bluebloods"?

For five hundred years beginning in the eighth century A.D., the Moors ruled large portions of southern Europe including Spain. The Spanish, originally a people of milky complexion, intermarried with the swarthy Moors, producing the darker-skinned Spanish people of today. However, certain of the Spanish aristocracy did not associate with the Moors but were allowed to live undisturbed in the mountains of Castile. Here, these venerable old families deliberately avoided the sun to preserve their light complexion and thus set themselves apart from the foreign invaders. As a result, their skin became very pale and, in the case of the older people, very translucent. This allowed blood vessels to show through the skin in vivid blue, which led to these pure, upper-class Castilians being referred to as "bluebloods."

When the English learned of this, they applied the same term to their own aristocracy, and the term "blueblood" became part of the English language.

Ever Wonder Why?

—stuffed furniture comes with tags that say "DO NOT REMOVE UNDER PENALTY OF LAW"?

At one time, manufacturers of stuffed furniture could not always be counted on to construct the furniture out of the proper materials. To protect consumers, state legislatures passed laws that stiffened the penalties for such deception and required that furniture manufacturers attach to each piece of stuffed furniture a tag informing the buyer of the exact materials used in the furniture's construction. These laws also made it illegal for *sellers* of furniture to remove the tag.

Therefore the warning "DO NOT REMOVE UNDER PENALTY OF LAW" applies only to sellers of furniture and not to consumers. For a long time, though, many consumers believed that the tag applied to them and were afraid to remove it. Because of this, the tag has now been modified to read "UNDER PENALTY OF LAW THIS TAG IS NOT TO BE REMOVED, EXCEPT BY THE CONSUMER."

—that painfully tender spot at the tip of the elbow is called the "funny bone"?

Actually, the funny bone is not a bone at all but a nerve. It is the ulnar nerve and it runs along a shallow groove in the ulna, the larger of the two forearm bones. The nerve gets very close to the surface at the tip of the elbow, and when it is struck there, it causes a sharp, shocking pain in the arm and hand.

For a while many people thought the pain was caused by striking the *upper* arm bone, and since the medical name for that bone is the *humerus*, someone decided it would be amusing to refer to it as the "humorous" or "funny" bone.

Ever Wonder Why?

—horseshoes are considered lucky?

In almost every country where there have been horses, horseshoes have been considered lucky. The reasons for this are varied, but the traditional explanation goes back to a tale told around the middle of the tenth century.

It is told that St. Dunstan, who was a blacksmith before he became archbishop of Canterbury, was approached one day in his blacksmith shop by Satan, who wanted to buy horseshoes for his cloven hooves. Dunstan, recognizing the devil immediately, told him that he, the devil, would have to be shackled to the wall before the shoes could be put on. Once the devil had been securely bound, Dunstan made the nailing on of the shoes so painful that the devil begged for mercy. Dunstan told the devil he would release him only if he promised never to enter the house of a Christian again. The devil quickly agreed but asked how he would recognize such a house. Dunstan thought for a moment, then held up a horseshoe. That would be the sign, he said, a horseshoe hung over the front door. Hence the lucky reputation of the horseshoe.

—stuffed eggs are called "deviled eggs"?

Because when stuffed eggs were first introduced, they were covered with pepper so hot that one bite brought to mind the fires of hell.

Ever Wonder Why?

—Rice Krispies go snap, crackle, pop?

Rice Krispies are made by steam-cooking kernels of rice in such a way that each kernel fills with tiny air bubbles and puffs up. The puffed-up kernels are flattened and then roasted until they become crisp. When milk is poured on Rice Krispies, each kernel gets wet and swells unevenly. This causes the crisp part of the kernels to give way and break with a snap, crackle, or pop.

—*X*s at the end of a letter signify kisses?

In the Middle Ages, when many people were unable to read or write, documents were often signed using an *X*. This *X*, or cross, was viewed by many as the sign of St. Andrew, and it represented a secret oath to fulfill the obligations specified in the document. In the same way many people now kiss the Bible when taking an oath, they then kissed the signature *X* to affirm their sincerity. Eventually the *X* and the kiss became synonymous and the *X* was used as a symbol for a kiss in correspondence.

—it is considered unlucky to light three cigarettes on one match?

The origin of this superstition goes back to the time when soldiers fought in trenches. In those days lighting "three on a match" could indeed prove very unlucky on the battlefield. If a match stayed lit long enough to light three cigarettes, it would give a night sniper time enough to take aim and fire at the lighted target.

Ever Wonder Why?

—the color red angers a bull?

Actually, the color red does not anger a bull since bulls are color-blind and can't tell red from any other color. In a bullfight it is the movement of the bullfighter's cape that makes the bull charge, not its color. This is why the bullfighter has to shake his cape to make the bull charge.

The idea that the color red angers a bull came from the custom in Spain of using red bullfighter capes. But this color was chosen to excite the spectators, not the bull. The color red has always had an exciting effect on humans, often causing an increase in blood pressure, a quickened pulse rate, and heightened anxiety. It has been suggested that this reaction to red may be due to its being the color of blood.

—frankfurters in a bun are called "hot dogs"?

In 1852 in Frankfurt, Germany, members of the butchers' guild created a long, thin sausage that they named "frank-furter" in honor of their town. One of these butchers owned a dachshund, and as soon as it was noticed that the shape of the sausage was the same as that of the dog, the sausages became known as "dachshund sausages." These dachshund sausages came to the United States under that name and were sold red-hot by various sausage peddlers. One of these peddlers, noticing that his sausages often burned his customers' fingers, decided to put them into buns. A *New York Times* cartoonist, T. A. Dargan, was very impressed with these hot dachshund sausages in buns and decided to illustrate them in a *New York Times* cartoon. However, Dargan wasn't sure about the spelling of "dachshund," so he called the sausages "hot dogs." As you know, the name caught on.

Ever Wonder Why?

—revealing a secret is said to be "letting the cat out of the bag"?

When the Muslims invaded southern Europe in the first part of the eighth century, they immediately passed a law forbidding the sale of pork. This was done because Muhammad, the founder of the Muslim religion, had declared pork to be unclean. This law, of course, didn't change the southern Europeans' love of pork, and there soon developed a black market for the meat. In secret transactions, usually conducted in the dead of night, farmers would sell to city dwellers suckling pigs concealed in large sacks or bags. Occasionally, a less than honest farmer would try to swindle a city buyer by selling a bag containing not a pig but a cat. If something went amiss and the bag came open during the transaction, this literally "let the cat out of the bag." This is why, today, revealing a secret is said to be "letting the cat out of the bag."

—onions make you cry?

When a fresh onion is sliced, a gas called propanethiol-S is released into the air. When this gas reaches the eye, it mixes with the water in the eye to form a weak acid. This acid irritates the eye and causes the tear-producing glands to flood the eye with water in an attempt to wash away the irritant. These tears make it appear that the person slicing the onion is crying.

Ever Wonder Why?

—cowboys wear such unique boots?

There are three characteristics of cowboy boots that make them unique. These are the pointed toe, the high heel, and the wide, unlaced top. The reasons for these are as follows: the pointed toe is to make it easy for the cowboy to insert his foot into the stirrup; the high heel is to enable his foot to get a firm hold on the stirrup; and the wide top is so the cowboy's foot can easily slip out of his boot if he falls off his horse in such a way that his boot gets caught in the stirrup.

—soft drinks are called "pop"?

Carbonated soft drinks—soft drinks charged under pressure with the gas carbon dioxide—were originally sold in bottles with corks. When the cork was removed and the pressure released, the gas escaped suddenly with a loud *pop*. This led to the drink being referred to as "pop."

—seagulls in a group at the beach always face the same direction?

Because of the way seagulls are built—heavy in the front and light in the back—they experience less wind resistance when they face into the wind. That is what they are doing when you see them at the beach on a windy day all facing the same direction. They are facing into the wind to reduce wind resistance.

—sellers of illegal whiskey are called "bootleggers"?

In the days of the Old West when it was against the law to sell alcohol to Indians, disreputable peddlers would sometimes smuggle alcohol onto Indian reservations by hiding flasks in the legs of their boots. These smugglers became known as "bootleggers," a term that now means anyone who sells illegal alcohol.

Ever Wonder Why?

—Mexican jumping beans jump?

In Chihuahua, Mexico, there grows a bean plant called Sabastiania Pavoniana that serves as a temporary home for a bean moth called Carpocapsa saltitans. When it comes time for the female bean moth to reproduce, she lays her eggs on the flower of the bean plant. As the plant grows, its fruit—a hard-shelled bean—forms around the eggs, completely enveloping them. As both bean and egg develop, the egg turns into a larva, which then feeds on the meat inside the bean. When the insides have been completely eaten away, the larva coats the walls of the bean with a silky substance and begins to batter the walls by contracting and expanding its body. It does this with such force that it causes the bean to jump and roll. Within a few months, the larva changes into a moth, pierces the weakened wall of the bean, and emerges.

—people say "God bless you" when you sneeze?

Dating back to biblical times, the sneeze was believed to be a sign of imminent personal danger to the sneezer. This was probably because a sneeze, in those days, was a symptom commonly associated with the plague. Therefore, when someone sneezed, it was believed that he or she was in need of immediate help from God. Thus began the custom of saying "God bless you" to a sneezer.

Ever Wonder Why?

—toy bears are called "teddy" bears?

The teddy bear was introduced in 1907, about the time when President Theodore "Teddy" Roosevelt, while on a bear hunt, came upon a baby bear that he refused to let anyone shoot. The president took a lot of ribbing about this, especially from the press, and one cartoonist for a national publication published a sketch depicting the incident. It was not long after this cartoon was published that toy manufacturers picked up on the idea and began marketing "teddy" bears.

—we cross our fingers for good luck?

Crossing one's fingers is a way of secretly making the sign of the cross, and it was done by early Christians to ask for divine assistance without attracting the attention of pagans.

—clothiers use those little plastic stems to attach price tags to their merchandise?

All merchants have had problems with dishonest customers switching price tags from less expensive items to more expensive ones, knowing that a busy cashier would probably not notice the difference. Clothiers have found that they can almost eliminate the problem by attaching their price tags with plastic stems. This is because tag switching cannot then be done without physically cutting the plastic stem, and this, of course, would make reattaching the tag impossible.

Ever Wonder Why?

—hamburger steak is sometimes called Salisbury steak?

After World War I a campaign was started to remove all German expressions from the English language. This meant finding a different name for hamburger steak, which had been named after the town of Hamburg, Germany. Someone soon recalled that an English physician named James H. Salisbury had once been a strong promoter of hamburger meat as a cure for a host of common diseases, and it was decided to rename the meat after him.

—radio and TV stations in the United States always use call letters beginning with *W* or *K*?

The equipment used by radio and TV stations to broadcast their programs is capable of transmitting over a wide range of frequencies. To make sure that these broadcasts do not interfere with each other, the government of each country tells each station which frequency it may use and assigns to it a unique call sign usually consisting of four letters. The station must then use this call sign periodically to identify its broadcasts and assigned frequencies.

Under an international agreement, each country has been allotted a specific series of four-letter call signs. For example, Japan was allotted all call signs beginning with the letter *J*, Canada all call signs beginning with the letter *B*, and France those beginning with the letter *C*. The United States was assigned two series of call signs: those beginning with *K* for stations west of the Mississippi and those beginning with *W* for stations east of the Mississippi. In order to receive a license from the FCC, all radio and TV stations in the United States must use call signs beginning with one of these two letters.

Ever Wonder Why?

—a person who peeps through a window is called a "peeping Tom"?

Before Lady Godiva made her famous ride through the streets of Coventry, England, she issued a proclamation asking that all of the townspeople remain indoors and keep their shutters closed during the ride. Everyone complied with her request except for Tom, the tailor. Tom bored a small hole through his shutter so that he could take a peek, and ever since that day has been known as Peeping Tom of Coventry. This, of course, is why peepers today are called "peeping Toms."

—aluminum foil is shiny on one side and dull on the other?

Aluminum foil is made by flattening blocks of aluminum into thin sheets and then passing these sheets between two highly polished steel rollers, two sheets at a time. The sides of the sheets that come into direct contact with the steel rollers emerge with a high shine; the two inner sides emerge with a dull finish. Therefore, the difference in the two sides of aluminum foil is just a result of the manufacturing process and has nothing to do with which side should be placed next to the food.

Ever Wonder Why?

—barbershops use red-white-and-blue poles as their symbol?

In the 1700s, barbers not only gave haircuts and shaves but also pulled teeth, performed minor surgery, and did bloodletting. During the bloodletting, patients were instructed to hold on to a pole in such a way as to cause the veins in their arms to swell and the blood to flow freely. This pole was usually painted red to hide the blood spatters, and when it was not in use, it was left outside to air. Around the pole were usually wrapped white bandages, which were also put out to air. This red-and-white combination soon came to symbolize barbershops. After barbers no longer did bloodletting, someone got the idea of using painted red-and-white poles as the barber's symbol. Blue was added to poles in America around 1900, probably to match the colors in our flag.

—the symbol ℞ is used on medical prescriptions?

It was once believed that ℞ stood for *recipere*, the Latin word for "take this." This explanation, however, did not account for the crossed foot on the symbol. A more likely explanation is one based on the sign of Jupiter.

In ancient times the god Jupiter was thought to have dominion over matters involving health and healing. Even today the period of planet Jupiter's ascendancy is believed by many to be a good time for gathering herbs and making medicine. It became customary, therefore, to precede medical prescriptions with the sign of Jupiter as a means of ensuring favorable results from the medicine. The sign of Jupiter is ♃, and over time this sign has been gradually distorted until it now takes the form of the familiar ℞.

Ever Wonder Why?

—a person who acts crazy is sometimes said to be "as mad as a hatter"?

Hat makers in the nineteenth century used mercury, a poison, in the manufacture of hats. This poison had an ill effect on employees who came in direct contact with it, making them shake, hallucinate, and do other strange things. Because of this, "hatters" during that period gained the reputation of being mad.

—ice cubes stick together in a glass?

Pressure causes ice to melt. In fact, this is what enables a glacier to move. The tremendous weight of the glacier causes the ice on the very bottom to melt, creating a layer of water on which the glacier glides.

When two ice cubes in a glass of water touch for a prolonged period, the slight pressure of one against the other causes a little bit of ice at the point of contact to melt. The melted water then flows away from the point of contact and immediately refreezes. This refrozen water forms a sort of "weld" that causes the ice cubes to stick together.

—the "not on Sunday" laws are referred to as "blue laws"?

In the early 1770s an Anglican rector named Samuel Peters fled to England after being accused of conspiring against the American colonies. In England he began to write about things gone wrong in the colonies, and in particular he alleged that, in Connecticut, there were in existence certain moral laws so strict that they forbade such things as kissing one's own wife on Sunday. Reverend Peters claimed that these laws were contained in a book bound in blue, and this led to these laws—and all subsequent never-on-Sunday laws—being called "blue laws."

Ever Wonder Why?

—your knuckles crack?

The bones in the finger are separated by small pads of cartilage, and in between these pads and the bones are small pockets of a thick liquid. When the fingers are bent, the bones pull away slightly from the pads of cartilage and a vacuum forms between the bone, the pad, and the surface of the liquid. As the bending continues and the bones are pulled farther apart, the surface tension of the liquid eventually gives way and the vacuum bubble bursts, making the cracking sound you hear. The process is very similar to what happens when you pull a rubber suction cup off a smooth surface.

—the lapels on men's coats have notches cut into them?

Lapels were originally put on suits so they could be turned up in cold weather to keep the neck warm. It became apparent, however, that a straight lapel large enough to protect the neck would be too large to lie flat against the chest when turned down. It was found that notches cut into the lapel would correct this problem and also make the collar fit more snugly around the neck.

The buttonhole in the lapel was once used to button the lapel in the "up" position.

—"lb." is used to represent pound?

Like much of our language, this comes from the Latin. It is a contraction of *libra*, the Latin word for pound.

Ever Wonder Why?

—ice cream and fruit concoctions
are called "sundaes"?

In the late nineteenth century local laws in many areas forbade the sale of ice cream sodas on the Sabbath, presumably because the sodas were too sinfully delicious. To attract the Sunday crowd ice cream parlors began serving ice cream topped with various kinds of fruit, advertising these concoctions as sodaless sodas. They were a big success, and soon people began to call them "Sundays." Later the parlors altered the spelling to "sundaes," hoping this would change the dish's image from a Sunday-only dessert to an everyday treat.

—people's teeth chatter when they get scared?

When a person experiences great fear, his or her body automatically prepares itself for defense. It does this, in part, by contracting certain muscles that will be needed if the person chooses to fight and certain other muscles he will need if he elects to flee instead.

Since the teeth and jaws were once primary means of defense, the body automatically gets these ready for action whenever a person is confronted with a threatening situation. It does this by contracting the muscles in the jaw, causing the jaw muscles to shiver. It is this shivering that makes the teeth chatter.

Similarly, the body contracts the muscles in the legs to prepare the person to run, and this causes the leg muscles to shiver. This is why some people's knees knock together when they are frightened.

Ever Wonder Why?

—the letters in traffic signs painted directly on the pavement are so large?

The letters have to be this large in order to be readable by approaching motorists. Motorists must be able to read the signs at distances of 50 feet or more and at an angle of about 20 degrees. When these letters are viewed under these conditions, they appear normal in size and are perfectly readable. To see this effect, tilt this page until you are viewing the word below at an angle of about 20 degrees.

—private detectives are called "private eyes"?

Around 1925 the Pinkerton Detective Agency adopted "we never sleep" as its motto. To symbolize this, the motto was shown over the picture of an ever-wakeful eye. It is this picture that led to private detectives being called "private eyes."

Ever Wonder Why?

—the keys on a typewriter are arranged so strangely?

The very first typewriters did not use the present-day key arrangement but instead used a straight alphabetic design reading left to right and top to bottom. However, a problem soon arose with this design because it placed the most frequently used keys close together, and when a fast typist used the machine, the printing spokes for these keys would get jammed. To correct the problem, an inventor named Christopher Sholes designed the current arrangement, which places the most frequently used keys further apart.

Ever Wonder Why?

**—children put on grotesque masks and go out
"trick or treating" on Halloween night?**

Since the seventh century A.D., Europeans have celebrated All Saints Day on November 1. This is a day to honor all saints, especially those who do not already have a special day in their name. Originally All Saints Day was known as All Hallows Day, the word *hallow* coming from an Anglo-Saxon word meaning holy. The night before All Hallows Day was, of course, All Hallows Eve. Over time, All Hallows Eve was shortened to just Hallows Eve and, eventually, distorted to Halloween.

The Druids, a group of Celtic religious priests in ancient Britain, celebrated Halloween on October 31. They believed that on that day, Saman, the Lord of the Dead, would summon together the souls of all the persons who had died during the past twelve months and encourage them to plot against the good people who would be honoring the saints on the following day. It was believed that these souls would take the form of grotesque animals and haunt the countryside, demanding gifts from the townspeople and threatening harm to anyone who refused. To defend themselves, the townspeople would gather on Halloween night, build bonfires, and keep careful watch for the malicious demons. Whenever gates were stolen, horses turned loose, or windows broken on that night, it was presumed to have been the work of these ghostly night wanderers.

Except in a few isolated villages in Europe, people no longer believe that Saman's spooky spirits lurk about on Halloween. The day has now become just a time to tell scary stories and play mischievous tricks on one's neighbors.

Thus, when a child dresses up like a monster on Halloween and goes out "trick or treating," the child is unknowingly pre-

Ever Wonder Why?

tending to be one of Saman's resurrected souls, haunting the town and demanding gifts from the frightened townspeople.

——something really tight is said to be as
"tight as Dick's hatband"?

Dick, in the above saying, is Richard Cromwell, son of Oliver Cromwell. The hatband is the English crown. When Richard tried to carry on the work of his father, who ruled England from 1649 to 1658, he was unsuccessful and was so severely ridiculed that he had to leave the office after one year. In those days it was said in derision that Dick's hatband, the English crown, was so tight that he couldn't make it stay on. Hence, the use of the term to describe anything or anybody really tight.

——a rabbit's foot is considered lucky?

The idea that rabbits are special animals dates back to western Europe before 600 B.C., a time when spirits were believed to inhabit the bodies of animals and when humankind itself was believed to have descended from certain sacred animals. The Celts, an ancient race living in Europe at that time, believed rabbits to be especially sacred for two reasons. First, the fact that rabbits spend so much time underground led the Celts to believe that they were communicating with numina, underground spirits who were thought to inhabit animals' bodies. And second, because rabbits are so prolific, it was believed that these spirits intended rabbits to be symbols of health, prosperity, and procreativity.

Therefore, any part of a rabbit was believed to be lucky, but since rabbits' feet are small and easily dried out, it was this part of the animal that most people carried for luck.

Ever Wonder Why?

—when someone dies, people often say that person "bought the farm"?

It is believed that this was first said about soldiers killed in action. Many soldiers from rural America frequently expressed their dream of going back home, buying a farm, and living a quiet life far from the horrors of the war. When such a young man was killed in action, it was sometimes said, ironically, that he had finally "bought the farm," meaning that he had finally achieved a peaceful existence.

—there is a best man at a wedding?

In days of old, when young men often went to neighboring villages to find their wives-to-be, it was not uncommon for a young man to encounter heavy resistance from the girl's kinfolk or perhaps her other suitors. To help overcome such resistance, a young man would take with him a strong and faithful friend. It was the job of this friend to help fend off attackers during the abduction and stand guard by the couple during the wedding. This friend became known as the groom's best man.

—trick candles keep relighting after you blow them out?

The wick of a trick candle contains small amounts of magnesium, and when you light the candle, you are also lighting the magnesium. When you blow out the flame, the magnesium inside of the wick continues to burn and, in a moment, relights the wick.

Ever Wonder Why?

—so many cows are named "Bossy"?

Apparently the person who first used this name around 1843 knew Latin, because it is believed that the name "Bossy" comes from the Latin word *bos* meaning cow or ox. So cows are named "Bossy" for the same reason that lions are often named "Leo."

—men's trousers have those seemingly useless cuffs?

In the late 1880s an English nobleman attended a high-society wedding in New York shortly after a rainstorm. When he arrived at the church, water was still standing in the streets, and before leaving his carriage, the Englishman turned up the bottoms of his trousers to keep them from getting wet. Once inside the church, he simply forgot to turn them down again. American guests at the wedding noticed the nobleman's turned-up trousers and took this to be the latest style from England. Soon American tailors began to receive orders for men's trousers with "cuffs."

—"to kick the bucket" means to die?

There are a number of explanations for the origin of this expression, but the most plausible one has to do with the way some people committed suicide in the past. It was once fairly common for a man bent on killing himself to do so by standing on an upturned bucket, putting a noose around his neck, and then "kicking the bucket."

—you never see cashew nuts in their shells?

Because their shells contain a strong acid that is capable of blistering the skin. The nut itself has to be roasted to make sure that all traces of the acid are removed.

Ever Wonder Why?

—rare events are said to occur
"once in a blue moon"?

Once in a blue moon is an appropriate way to describe a rare event, because blue moons are, themselves, rare but actual occurrences.

A blue moon can occur when large quantities of dust or other fine debris travel high enough into the atmosphere to filter the moon's reflected light. One such blue moon occurred in 1883 when a volcanic eruption on the island of Krakatoa spewed volcanic dust thirty miles into the air. This dust, which spread three thousand miles, filtered the moon's light, making it appear pale blue. As recently as 1950, another blue moon occurred when a forest fire along the Alaskan highway in northern Canada sent smoke, dust, and sulfur high into the atmosphere. For many days the people of Great Britain witnessed a blue moon.

Thus, events that can occur, but only under the rarest of circumstances, are well described by the phrase "once in a blue moon."

—Dalmatians are the traditional
mascots of firehouses?

Long before Dalmatians became firehouse mascots, they were bred as coach dogs. Coach dogs were trained to run alongside horse-drawn carriages to help guard against highwaymen. Because of the Dalmatian's ability to run long distances, its inbred love of horses, and its vivid coloring, it was a natural choice as the dog to run ahead of the horse-drawn fire engine of the past, warning onlookers to clear the way. After the fire engine was motorized and the Dalmatian was no longer needed for its services, firemen honored the breed by adopting it as the firehouse mascot.

Ever Wonder Why?

—we play April fool jokes on people on April 1?

Until the middle of the sixteenth century, the European new year began on March 25, the day that marked the beginning of spring. To celebrate the new year, festivities involving much gift-giving and partygoing were held for seven days, culminating on April 1. Around 1564 King Charles IX of France changed the calendar, moving the beginning of the new year to January 1. Many people who either didn't get the word or simply refused to honor the change continued to exchange gifts and hold parties on April 1. Because of this, they were called April fools and were mocked by others, who sent them frivolous presents, invited them to nonexistent parties, and played other pranks on them. Eventually, people just pretended to go through the rituals and the day became just a day for pranks.

—people say "the coast is clear" to mean that no one is looking?

This expression originated with seagoing smugglers during Shakespeare's time, and it originally meant that no one was guarding the coast, so it was safe to sail on in.

—shifting responsibility to someone else is called "passing the buck"?

In card games, such as poker, it was once customary to pass an item, called a buck, from player to player to indicate whose turn it was to deal. The name "buck" probably came from the fact that a silver dollar was often the item passed around. If a player did not wish to assume the responsibility of dealing, he would simply "pass the buck" to the next player.

Ever Wonder Why?

—you get more colds in cold weather?

Exposing the body to low temperatures will not, in itself, bring on the common cold. Colds are caused by viruses. However, the particular viruses that most often cause colds tend to flourish best at low temperatures. Therefore, in cold weather these viruses grow and multiply more rapidly in the body and eventually produce the common cold symptoms.

—some china is called bone china?

Because powdered animal bone is mixed with the clay used to make this kind of china to give it a special translucency, strength, and whiteness.

—we say something is "brand" new?

The word *brand*, as it is used here, means fresh from the fire, as might be said of something recently made in a forge. In fact, in Shakespeare's day, the term was actually "fire new."

—people clink their glasses before drinking a toast?

In less civilized times it was not uncommon for someone to try to kill a supposed enemy by offering him a poisoned drink. To prove to a guest that a drink was, in fact, safe, it became customary for a host to hold out his own glass and allow the guest to pour a small amount of his drink into it. Both men would then take a drink simultaneously. When a guest wished to show that he trusted his host, he would not pour the liquid but would simply touch the host's glass with his own. The clinking of glasses before a toast is what remains of this ritual.

Ever Wonder Why?

—so many men in the South are called "Bubba"?

Bubba is a corrupted form of the word *brother*. It is used as a pet name and pronounced as a small child might say "brother." In the South, where the term originated, it is a term of endearment and usually applies to an older brother, one to whom the other children might look up to for guidance and protection.

—to "86" something means to cancel or put an end to it?

In fact, "86" is one of many codes once used by soda-fountain employees to communicate quickly among themselves. Code 19 meant a banana split, code 33 meant a cherry-flavored Coke, and code 86 meant "we're out of that item." Therefore, if a cook "86'd" an order, it meant he was canceling it.

—chefs wear those tall, funny hats?

First of all, health regulations in most states require that chefs in public food establishments wear hats of some sort to keep their hair from falling into the food. Chefs have chosen hats that are tall and ballooned at the top because this design allows air to circulate around the scalp and help keep it cool in kitchens where temperatures can get very high. The hats are usually white because undyed (white) fabric is considered more sanitary than colored fabric.

Ever Wonder Why?

—stock prices are quoted in eighths of a dollar?

In the eighteenth century the American dollar was officially equated in value to the Spanish silver dollar, a coin so large that it was frequently divided into eight parts. Because of this, fractions of the American dollar were, for a long time, also expressed in eighths, especially by the Europeans with whom Americans traded. When the stock market was established toward the end of the eighteenth century, stock prices were quoted in dollars and eighths of a dollar, and the practice never changed.

—soldier uniforms, once very colorful, are today dull and drab?

Up until the Napoleonic wars, military uniforms were indeed brightly colored, but the method of warfare began to change at about that time. When soldiers attacked each other with swords and lances, brightly colored uniforms made little difference, but as firearms became more accurate at long distances, uniforms had to be made less colorful so as not to present too good a target for enemy marksmen. Hence, the emergence of drab uniforms.

—fish is often called brain food?

Two nineteenth-century German chemists, Jacob Moleschott and Ludwig Buchner, believed they had determined phosphorus to be the primary chemical element required for all mental activity. In fact, they proclaimed "no phosphorus, no thought." Since it had already been established that fish are very rich in phosphorus, a naturalist named Louis Agassiz put the two ideas together and concluded that eating fish is good for the brain.

It has since been determined that phosphorus is no more essential to mental activity than a number of other elements.

Ever Wonder Why?

—you can sometimes see a star out of the corner of your eye but not when you look directly at it?

Light images entering the eye come in through the lens and are focused on the retina located at the back of the eyeball. On the retina there are two kinds of light-sensitive cells: cones that sense color and rods that sense brightness. Directly behind the lens, in the center of the field of vision, there are both rods and cones. But a few degrees away from the center, there are mostly rods, and these rods are more numerous and more densely packed than those at the center. This means that the area of the retina away from the center of the field of vision is more capable of detecting faint light images than those at dead center. Thus, when a very dim light comes in through the corner of the eye, it strikes these densely packed rods and is seen. But when the eye is turned directly toward the light source, the light strikes the central portion of the retina where there are fewer rods, and the object seems to vanish.

—judges wear black robes?

Judges' robes were not always black. They were very colorful until the death of Queen Mary II in 1694. At that time, they were changed to black to mourn her death and were just never changed back.

Ever Wonder Why?

—someone who takes back a gift is called an "Indian giver"?

Early American colonists used the term *Indian* to describe something they considered a poor substitute for the real thing as they had known it in England. This led to expressions like Indian summer, Indian tea, and Indian corn, where the word *Indian* meant bogus.

Since Indians once had the reputation of giving gifts, not for the pleasure of giving, but because they expected to get something in return, their giving was not considered genuine, and was, therefore, called "Indian giving." Later, anyone who gave a gift and then took it back was said to be an Indian giver.

—a man tips his hat to greet a lady?

In the days of chivalry, a knight raised the visor on his helmet to show peaceful intentions. It, therefore, became customary for a knight to raise his visor when a lady approached. As helmets got smaller and lighter, the custom changed to raising the entire helmet. It is this custom that has come down to us as tipping one's hat to a lady.

—a flag at half-mast is used as a gesture of respect for a recently departed?

Warships of old flew their colors—the ship's flag—at the top of the ship's mast. After a naval battle it used to be customary for the defeated ship to lower its flag to half-mast to make room for the victor's flag above it. After this was no longer the custom, a lowered flag continued to be a universal sign of respect. It was used by ships passing at sea as a friendly salute, and eventually it became a gesture of respect for a worthy departed.

Ever Wonder Why?

—a ship's speed is expressed in knots?

One knot means one nautical mile per hour. One nautical mile is approximately 6,076 feet (the distance equivalent to $\frac{1}{60}$ of a degree at the equator). A simple calculation will show that, if you are traveling at 1 nautical mile per hour, you are traveling $47\frac{1}{4}$ feet every 28 seconds. And, of course, if you are traveling at $47\frac{1}{4}$ feet every 28 seconds, you are traveling at 1 nautical mile per hour. Sailors of old used this relationship to measure a ship's speed. Each ship carried a light rope, called a log line, with a wood float and weight attached to one end and with knots tied in it every $47\frac{1}{4}$ feet. To measure the ship's speed, the end of the line with the float would be placed in the water. As the ship moved forward, the line would be pulled off of a reel at a certain speed. If 1 knot was being pulled off the reel every 28 seconds, the ship was traveling 1 nautical mile per hour, or 1 knot. If 6 knots were being pulled off the reel every 28 seconds, the speed was 6 nautical miles per hour, or 6 knots, and so on.

**—admitting you are wrong is said
"eating humble pie"?**

When a deer was killed in eleventh-century E..... ..., it was customary to give the deer's best and tenderest parts to the hunter who killed it, his eldest son, and his best male friends. To the wife, children, and other friends of the hunter were left the less desirable parts—the heart, kidneys, entrails, etc. These parts were called the deer's "umbles," and to improve their taste they were usually cooked in a pie. Eating the pie was clearly a sign of lower status, so if someone committed an error and had to apologize, it was jokingly suggested that until he learns better, he should be "eating umble pie." Over time, "umble" somehow became "humble."

—liquor is sometimes called "hooch"?

When America acquired Alaska in 1876, the territory was placed under military command and a law was passed prohibiting the sale of liquor to the native Alaskans. So the Alaskans learned to make liquor on their own out of brown sugar, flour, and fruit. This was a very strong liquor, and it was first made in a little village called Hoochinoo near Sitka, Alaska. The Alaskans called the liquor "hoochinoo," but during the Klondike gold rush, the name was shortened to "hooch." Today the term applies to any liquor but especially to bad or strong liquor.

Ever Wonder Why?

—the depth of water is measured in fathoms?

The fathom came about quite naturally since it is based upon a dimension of the human body. The word *fathom* comes from an Anglo-Saxon word meaning "embrace" or "outstretched arms," and one fathom is roughly the distance between the fingertips of a man's outstretched arms. To use this as a measure of water depth, a weighted line was lowered into the water until it touched bottom and then pulled up again. The length of line that had been under water was then measured by repeatedly stretching the lines between outstretched arms. If this could be done eight times, the depth was eight fathoms, and so on.

Of course, the actual distance between a man's fingertips would vary with the size of the man, so the fathom was eventually set at six feet.

—doughnuts have holes?

The doughnut was invented in 1847 by a New England sea captain named Hanson Gregory. Some say that Captain Gregory put holes in his doughnuts to permit a more thorough cooking of the dough, thereby making the doughnut more digestible. Others say that he put the holes there so that he could hook a few of the doughnuts on the handles of his ship's steering wheel to have them close at hand while piloting the ship. Take your choice.

—people cross their hearts to show sincerity?

The crossing gesture represents the holy cross, and when people cross their hearts, they are calling upon Christ as a witness to the truth of what they are saying.

Ever Wonder Why?

—golfers shout "fore" before they tee off?

"Fore" originally meant "get out of the way or you'll be shot." It is an old military term once used to warn the front row of riflemen to kneel down so that the second row could fire over their heads. The term was originally "Beware before," then it became "before" and finally it was shortened to just "fore."

—we get goose bumps?

Goose bumps are a carryover from ancient times when our ancestors had bodies covered with fur. Goose bumps are caused by the contraction of tiny muscles at the base of each strand of body hair, and when these muscles contract, they cause the hair to puff up. This served two purposes in the past. First, it created an insulating layer of air next to the skin that helped keep the body warm in cold weather. This is why goose bumps form when you get cold. Second, it gave our furry ancestors a larger and more menacing appearance in the face of danger, and this is why you get goose bumps when you are frightened.

Ever Wonder Why?

**—when something goes wrong, we say
"There'll be the devil to pay"?**

The devil in this expression is not Satan, and "to pay" has nothing to do with the usual definition of the term.

The devil is a seam on a wooden ship that is usually below the waterline and hard to reach. "To pay" means to caulk the seam with a water-resistant preparation like hot pitch. In order to get to the seam, a ship often had to be careened on a shallow bottom. When the tide went out, the work could be done, but it had to be done quickly before the tide came back in. If the ship were made ready, but the crew had not prepared the hot pitch, then they had "the devil to pay and no pitch hot."

**—someone in a precarious situation is said to be
"between the devil and the deep blue sea"?**

The devil is the same hard-to-reach seam mentioned above. To caulk the seam, a sailor often had to be suspended by rope under the hull of the ship just above the water while the ship was careened.

While caulking the seam, the sailor was in a dangerous position and was said to be "between the devil and the deep blue sea."

Ever Wonder Why?

—we measure lengths in inches, feet, and yards?

Like many of our other units of measure, these three resulted from man's early tendency to measure things with parts of his body. The inch came from the approximate width of a man's thumb, which was used to measure small distances. The foot is, of course, based upon the length of a man's foot, which he used to step off longer distances. The yard is about the distance between the tip of a man's nose and the fingers of his outstretched arm, a distance that became a standard for measuring lengths of cloth. Of course, since human dimensions vary as they do, more precise definitions were eventually established.

Other units of measure based on human dimensions are the (a) cubit, the distance from the elbow to the tip of the longest finger; (b) the digit, the width of a finger; (c) the fathom, the distance between the fingertips of outstretched arms, which is still used to measure water depths; and (d) the hand, the width of a four-finger hand, which is still used to measure the height of horses.

—when someone wants to caution you not to believe something too quickly, he or she says, "Take it with a grain of salt"?

Salt has long been believed to possess great purifying powers, and Pompey is said to have made it a practice to add a grain of salt to any drink suspected of containing poison. From this may have come the idea that one should accept certain suspicious offerings "with a grain of salt," that is, with a measure of caution.

Ever Wonder Why?

—yellow means cowardly?

Long before the Civil War there were two opposing sides on the issue of slavery. As debate between them heated up, agitators on both sides began publishing anonymous pamphlets that attacked public figures. The unsigned pamphlets, which typically contained vicious lies and insinuations, were usually printed on cheap, unbleached paper that had a yellowish tint. When it was learned that certain newspaper editors were taking part in the publishing of such pamphlets, the practice became known as "yellow journalism." Eventually, "yellow" came to mean any cowardly act.

Ever Wonder Why?

——wagon wheels in movies sometimes seem to turn backwards?

To see why this happens, assume that a wagon wheel with eight identical spokes is turning at such a rate that every twenty-fourth of a second the spokes of the wheel happen to line up in the same eight positions.

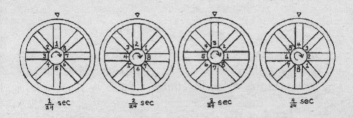

$\frac{1}{24}$ sec $\frac{2}{24}$ sec $\frac{3}{24}$ sec $\frac{4}{24}$ sec

Now suppose that a movie camera is filming the turning wheel at the rate of twenty-four frames per second. At this rate the camera will take a picture of the wheel every twenty-fourth of a second. But since the spokes of the wheel are in the same eight positions every twenty-fourth of a second, it will appear to the camera that the wheel is not moving. And when the film is shown, what the viewer will see is a wagon rolling along on wheels that are not turning. Everyone who watches old westerns has seen this happen on stagecoach wheels.

Assume now that the turning wheel is slowed down a bit so that the spokes do not quite reach the position indicated above by the time the camera takes its second picture, but are just to the left of it. When the camera takes its picture, the spokes are located just a little before where they were on the preceding picture. On all successive pictures, the spokes continue to move back little by little in this fashion.

51

Ever Wonder Why?

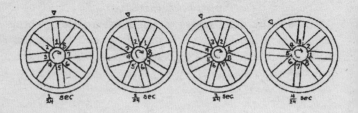

Since this sequence of pictures is all the camera sees, it appears to the camera—and to the people who view the movie—that the wheel is turning backwards.

—most traffic signs and markers are yellow?

Yellow is the most visible of all the colors in the spectrum. It can be seen from the farthest distance and it is conspicuous in all lighting conditions. This makes it a natural choice for traffic signs, which must be seen from great distances.

—stop signs are red?

While yellow is the most visible color in the spectrum, red is the most exciting. The color red elevates the blood pressure, increases the pulse rate, and heightens nervous tension. This makes red the color most likely to attract human attention, and this is exactly what is needed for stop signs.

It has been speculated that the color red has this effect because it is the color of human blood. Humans have been conditioned over millions of years to react strongly to the sight of blood as a sign that something is very wrong.

Ever Wonder Why?

—the cobra doesn't strike the snake charmer?

It is not the flute music that keeps the cobra from striking, because a cobra is stone deaf. The snake does have an auditory nerve, but it cannot detect sound. It can only sense vibrations from the ground.

The snake used by most snake charmers is not the aggressive king cobra, which is quick to strike at almost anything, but the asiatic cobra, a much quieter snake and one less likely to strike at a large target, especially one too large for it to eat. Even so, the snake charmer takes no chances, and so keeps his hands and the flute in constant motion so that the snake can never quite get into position to strike.

—ships are referred to as "she"?

Long ago, new sailing ships were dedicated to a goddess who supposedly protected the ship and guided it safely to its destination. An image of the goddess was usually carved on the ship's bow, and this carved image led to the ship's being referred to as "she."

Ever Wonder Why?

—high-flying jets leave a trail of white behind them?

The white trail that you see is, in fact, a man-made cloud.

At low altitudes where temperature and barometric pressure are high, the air is able to absorb and hold large quantities of water. But at high altitudes, where temperature and pressure are low, the air is unable to hold all of the water it absorbed at lower altitudes. At such high altitudes, water has a tendency to come out of the air (or condense), and when this happens a cloud is formed. But in order for this to happen, the air must contain small particles—such as dust—on which the water can condense. It also helps the process if the air is shaken or agitated.

At high altitudes the air is very clean and contains little or no dust. This means that under normal conditions the water that comes out of the air forms wispy clouds.

Now enter the high-flying jet. Its exhaust fills the airspace directly behind the plane with a huge supply of spent fuel particles, and at the same time it shakes or agitates the air. These are the proper conditions to cause the water particles to condense, and they do, leaving a long, narrow cloud across the sky in the plane's wake.

—people say "It's raining cats and dogs"?

In seventeenth-century England, hundreds of cats and dogs ran wild through streets that had little or no storm drainage. During heavy downpours many of these wild animals drowned, and their bodies would be seen floating in the torrents that raced through the streets. This gave the appearance that it had, literally "rained cats and dogs," and this led to the current expression.

Ever Wonder Why?

—when people spill salt they toss a few grains over their left shoulders?

Since salt purifies and preserves, it was considered holy in many cultures of the past. It was used in sacrifices and other religious rites, and it is still used today in Catholic baptismal rituals.

To upset a container of salt was believed to be an omen of approaching evil. To counteract the evil, the spiller of the salt had only one option—toss a few grains of the purifying salt into the face of the approaching evil.

But why over the left shoulder? Evil has always been associated with the left. For instance, the word *sinister* comes from the Latin word for left. It was believed that the impending evil due to the spilled salt would approach the spiller from behind and from the left. Hence the custom of tossing salt over the left shoulder.

—your palms sweat when you get nervous?

Palms sweat very easily because they contain more sweat glands than other parts of the body. The reason for this, it is assumed, goes back to the days when our ancestors climbed trees to get away from danger. Fear of the danger activated the sweat glands, making the palms moist, and this moisture provided our ancestors with a better grip when climbing trees.

As in the case of the prehensile tail, goose bumps, and body hair, sweaty palms no longer serve any useful purpose but are still with us even after millions of years of evolution.

Ever Wonder Why?

—most manholes are round?

Manholes are round because if they were any other shape, their covers might easily fall through the hole. If manholes were square, rectangular, oval, or any shape other than round, it would be possible to turn the cover so that its width would be less than one dimension of the hole, and this would enable the cover to fall through.

This can't happen with round manholes since the width (or diameter) of the circle measures the same in all directions.

Of course, any shape could be used if the cover is enough larger than the opening of the manhole. The round manhole just permits the smallest cover.

—the person sitting next to the driver in a car is said to be "riding shotgun"?

This seat, to the right of the driver, is where the guard on a stagecoach sat in the days of the Old West. Since this guard was usually armed with a shotgun, the person in this seat was said to be "riding shotgun." The term—probably heard in a Wild West movie—has been carried over to describe the seat next to the driver in an automobile.

—the sky is blue?

Sunlight, which we see as white light, is actually a mixture of the colors red, orange, yellow, green, blue, and purple. When sunlight passes through the earth's atmosphere, these colors are deflected and scattered in many different ways by atmospheric molecules and other matter in the air. The colors blue and purple are deflected the most, causing these colors to scatter all over the sky. Because the human eye can detect blue much more readily than purple, it is blue we see when we look up into the sky.

Ever Wonder Why?

—sailor suits are made the way they are?

The large bell-bottomed trousers were designed to make it easy for a sailor to roll up his pants when swabbing the deck and also to make it easier for him to slip out of his wet uniform if he finds himself in the water.

The cap is designed for easy storage and to serve as a flotation device. It is made of canvas and is almost airtight when soaking wet. When the cap is thoroughly wet and the brim turned down, it can be used to capture an air bubble and keep the sailor afloat.

Some say that the large flat collar that lies across the back of the uniform was to protect the main part of the uniform from the tar and powder that early sailors used to put on their pigtails.

—we have leap years?

We say there are 365 days in the year and by this we mean that it takes the earth 365 days to make its annual trip around the sun. Actually, though, it takes the earth 365¼ days to make this trip. This means that every year we gain one-fourth of a day and every four years we gain one full day. If we did nothing about this, our calendar would move backward one full day every four years relative to our seasons.

To keep this from happening, we capture the extra day every four years and put it into our smallest month, February.

Ever Wonder Why?

—people in the public eye are said to be "in the limelight"?

Limelight refers to a system of lighting invented in 1825 by a British army officer named Thomas Drummond. Drummond's light was called "limelight" because it was produced by burning a cylinder of lime (calcium oxide) in an oxyhydrogen flame. As the lime was oxidized by the flame, it produced an intense, brilliant light that could be directed into a beam by a glass lens.

Drummond's light was originally used to make distant survey stations more visible at night, but later it was also used in lighthouses and for stage lighting. In the theater it was used as a spotlight to direct the audience's attention to the most important activities taking place onstage. Performers in this light were said to be "in the limelight," and when the expression passed into general usage, it meant anyone at the center of public attention.

Ever Wonder Why?

——people say "mind your p's and q's" when they want you to be careful?

There are two equally plausible explanations for this saying. The first deals with the problems children have with the alphabet.

When children write letters, they sometimes get their lowercase p's and q's mixed up and write words like cuqboard and puit instead of cupboard and quit. To help them avoid such mistakes, teachers of old used to admonish them to "mind their p's and q's."

The second explanation traces the origin back to old English pubs where the number of pints and quarts of ale consumed by a patron were kept on a chalkboard under the headings p's and q's. When a patron had accumulated a high number of marks, he was reminded by the barkeeper to "mind his p's and q's."

——we nod our heads for "yes" and shake it for "no"?

The best explanation for this comes from Charles Darwin, who related these gestures to a baby's nursing habits. The forward head motion, or nod, is supposedly a breast-seeking pattern while shaking the head from side to side is a breast-rejecting motion. That is, in the first instance, the baby is saying "yes" and in the second it is saying "no." This is confirmed by the fact that a baby born deaf and blind will nod for "yes" and shake its head for "no."

Ever Wonder Why?

**—reprimanding someone is called
"reading him the riot act"?**

Our sovereign Lord the king chargeth and commandeth all persons being assembled immediately to disperse themselves and peacefully to depart to their habitations or to their lawful business, upon the pains contained in the act made in the first year of King George for preventing tumultuous and riotous assemblies. God save the King.

The above proclamation is the Riot Act as enacted in 1715 by the British Parliament under George I. Or, more correctly, it is what the Riot Act says must be read by the sheriff or mayor to disperse unlawful assemblages.

This is what reading the Riot Act originally meant. Today, of course, it has been distorted to mean giving anyone a severe reprimand.

—you don't see more houseflies in the winter?

Low temperatures, especially below freezing, are fatal to adult flies. The few flies you do see in the winter have survived in the larva or pupa state.

—laundry smells better when it is dried outside?

Sunlight, through a process called photolysis, breaks down compounds in laundry that cause odor, such as oil and perspiration absorbed from the body. The process doesn't remove the compounds but makes them less odorous.

Ever Wonder Why?

—illegal whiskey is called "moonshine"?

It was once supposed that this term was first applied to the making of illegal whiskey by moonlight in the mountains of Kentucky, Virginia, North Carolina, and Tennessee. In fact, the term is much older than that and was originally used to describe the smuggling of illegal brandy into England from France by moonlight.

—builders put a small tree on the top of a building as soon as its top frame is completed?

In ancient times the success of building projects was believed to depend more on the mood of the gods than on the builders' skill. To appease the gods and drive away evil spirits, the builders would attach plants thought to be inhabited by good spirits to the tops of their buildings as soon as the frames were completed. These plants, often decorated with flowers, ribbons, and strings of eggs, were supposed to lend their life-giving powers to the buildings and show that the buildings were as safe and solid as the ground in which the plants once grew.

Builders today still observe this superstition by placing a small tree on the top frame of a new building. The custom is called "topping out."

Ever Wonder Why?

—the bureaucratic process is often referred to as "red tape"?

The term "red tape" was made famous in the 1900s by Thomas Carlyle, who charged the English government with "red tapism." He was referring to the government's practice in those days of binding official papers in red ribbon. Since a matter having to go through government channels could be slowed down by the tying and untying of stacks of such bound documents, the process became known, unaffectionately, as "going through red tape."

—a wedding ring is always worn on the third finger?

It was once believed that a vein of blood ran directly from the third finger on the left hand to the heart. The vein was called *vena amoris*, or the vein of love, and early writings on matrimonial procedure suggested that it would be appropriate for one's wedding ring to be worn on that special finger.

—military men greet each other with a salute?

In the days of chivalry, a knight would greet a friend by raising his visor to expose his face. When visors went out of existence, men raised their hats for the same purpose. In the military this custom was eventually abbreviated to just touching the brim of the hat, leading to the present-day salute.

—special days are called "red letter" days?

This expression comes from the custom in the Christian church of showing special days in red letters on church calendars. It is believed that red letters were first used in the Book of Common Prayer in the church of England.

Ever Wonder Why?

—portholes on a ship are round?

The constant up-and-down motion of a ship puts considerable stress on the ship's skin, or outer covering. If portholes were designed with angles, this stress would tend to concentrate at those points and perhaps crack the skin. With round portholes such stress is evenly distributed around the holes, making it less likely for such cracks to occur.

—a thing that is no longer as good as it was is said to have "gone to pot"?

When a leftover dish is no longer suitable to be served alone, as an entree, it is often tossed into a pot for stew. Thus, such a dish has "gone to pot."

—tennis balls are fuzzy?

The fuzz slows down the ball in flight, keeps it from bouncing too high, and lets the racket get a better "grip" on it. A perfectly smooth ball would travel so fast and bounce so high that the game would be unplayable. Also, with a smooth ball, it would be much more difficult for the player to control the direction of the shots.

—a ten-dollar bill is called a "sawbuck"?

A sawbuck is another name for a carpenter's sawhorse. The fact that the end of a sawbuck looks like an X, the Roman numeral for 10, gave someone the idea of calling the ten-dollar bill a "sawbuck."

Ever Wonder Why?

—you can tear a newspaper smoothly from top to bottom but not from side to side?

Newsprint is, of course, made from fine wood pulp. In a newspaper the tiny fibers of wood are arranged so that most of them are aligned from top to bottom. Therefore, when you tear a piece of newspaper vertically, you are tearing with the grain and the tear is smooth. When you tear it from side to side, you are tearing against the grain, so you get jagged edges.

But why are the fibers aligned vertically? This is a result of the way paper is made. The tiny fibers are mixed with water and dropped onto a moving conveyor belt. As each fiber lands on the belt, it is jerked in the direction of the belt's movement and this results in most of the fibers being aligned in this direction. As the fibers come off the conveyor, they are dried into sheets and put into huge rolls. When these rolls are used for newspapers, the pages are cut so that the fibers are aligned vertically.

—someone is called a "son of a gun"?

Today the expression is used in a friendly, joking manner, but originally it had a quite different meaning.

There was a time when women were allowed to live on board naval ships, and it is said that when secret rendezvous took place between these women and the ship's crew, the meeting place was usually behind a canvas screen near the midship gun. Therefore, when a male child of uncertain parentage was born aboard the ship, he was entered in the ship's log as a "son of a gun."

Ever Wonder Why?

—so many military uniforms have a stripe down the side of each pant leg?

At one time military trousers were made to fit so tightly that buttons down the sides of legs were needed to enable the wearer to get his feet through. To hide these buttons, tailors began putting strips of cloth—usually of a different color—over them. This led to the idea of stripes on military trousers.

—breaking a mirror is said to lead to seven years of bad luck?

Centuries ago many believed that a person's image in a mirror was a reflection of that person's soul. That is why the legendary vampire, who had no soul, casts no reflection in a mirror. To the people who held this belief, breaking a mirror meant preventing a part of the soul from reuniting with its body. The absence of a portion of the soul, it was believed, would certainly lead to ill fortune. But why seven years? This goes back to a Roman belief that a person's health and fortune changed every seven years.

—cowboy hats are called "ten gallon" hats?

One account attributes this term to the fact that cowboys used their hats as water buckets to take water to their horses and to douse fires.

Another says the "gallon" comes from the spanish word *galon* meaning braid. Apparently the custom of decorating the base of the crown of the hat with a leather strip containing ten braids, or *galons*, led to the hat being called a "ten-gallon hat."

Ever Wonder Why?

—the letter *X* is used to represent the unknown?

The Arabic word used to represent an unknown quantity was *shei*. This was transcribed in Greek to *Xei* and later shortened to just *X*.

—people say "Let's talk turkey" when they want to get down to serious business?

The expression "talk turkey" is believed to have been explained in a report issued by the U.S. Engineers Department in 1848, which included the following account:

Today I heard an anecdote that accounts for one of our common sayings. It is related that a white man and an Indian went hunting, and afterwards, when they came to divide the spoils, the white man said, "You may take the buzzard and I will take the turkey, or I will take the turkey and you may take the buzzard." The Indian replied, "You never once said turkey to me."

—the wires strung between telephone poles sometimes hum?

It is not electricity that makes the wires hum. The hum is caused by the wind passing through the wires and vibrating them to make a sound that varies in pitch depending upon the speed of the wind and the tightness of the wire.

Ever Wonder Why?

—an expensive but nonproductive possession is called a "white elephant"?

This is said to have originated with the king of Siam, who supposedly gave white elephants to members of his court he wished to ruin. White elephants, at that time, were considered sacred and were not allowed to do work, yet they still had to be fed and cared for. Thus a possession that must be maintained at high cost but that offers no productive output in return is said to be a "white elephant."

—eating spicy foods sometimes makes people perspire?

Spicy foods, such as chili peppers, contain a chemical that stimulates the same nerve endings in the mouth as does a rise in temperature. These nerves, not knowing the difference, send a message to the brain telling it that the temperature near the face has risen. The brain reacts by activating cooling mechanisms to reduce the temperature around the face, and one of these mechanisms is perspiration.

Ever Wonder Why?

—that square enclosure used by boxers is called a "ring"?

In the early days of professional fistfighting, groups of fighters would travel from town to town challenging the local men. The fighters would arrange a few of the spectators in a circle and have them hold a ring of rope. Any man wishing to challenge one of the boxers would "toss his hat into the ring." The bout would then take place in this early boxing "ring."

As the number of spectators increased, the hand-held ring no longer sufficed, and it became necessary to fashion an enclosure by attaching ropes to stakes driven into the ground. Four stakes were normally used, which produced a square enclosure, but it continued to be called a boxing ring.

—the dead in Europe used to be buried with their heads to the west?

At one time it was believed that this practice, which was prevalent in northern Europe up until a century ago, was to ensure that on Judgment Day the dead would rise facing Jesus, who would arrive from the east. According to Matthew 24:27, "For as the lightning cometh out of the east, and shineth even unto the west; so shall also the coming of the Son of man be." However, this custom predates Christianity by several hundred years. It is now believed that the practice originated with early sun worshipers who wanted their resurrected to be facing the rising sun.

Ever Wonder Why?

—an exciting ball game is called a "barn burner"?

The original "barn burners" were an overzealous, anti-slavery faction of the Democratic party in the mid 1800s. They were so violently opposed to the proslavery faction of the party that, reportedly, they would burn down the whole barn (where the Democratic jackasses were kept) just to get rid of the rats (the proslavery Democrats). After this, any high excitement competition was often called a "barn burner."

—the mortarboard graduation cap is built the way it is?

The mortarboard is a modification of the four-cornered, ecclesiastic biretta worn by cardinals and bishops. The biretta is an acknowledged symbol of mastership and an appropriate cap for graduates. For academic purposes, the crown of the cap was enlarged to such an extent that it required some form of support to keep it from falling down on the face. This support took the form of a square piece of cardboard. With subsequent modifications the crown became flat and square, like the cardboard, and a skull cap was fitted underneath.

Of course, the cap is called a mortarboard because it resembles the square board masons use to carry mortar.

—ships and aircraft in trouble use "mayday" as their call for help?

This comes from the French *m'aidez*, which means "help me" and which is pronounced "mayday."

Ever Wonder Why?

—the sky is usually cloudless in the morning?

Clouds are formed when moist air is carried aloft by warm air currents rising from the earth's surface during the day. When this air reaches high altitudes where the temperature and barometric pressure are lower than at the earth's surface, the moisture comes out of the rising air and forms the water droplets we see as clouds. These clouds are very short-lived, though, and they usually disappear within minutes after they are formed as their water droplets mix with drier air and evaporate. Thus, during the daytime, clouds are continually being formed and then evaporated.

At night, when the surface of the earth cools, the cloud-producing process cuts off. The existing clouds continue to evaporate, but they are not replaced by new ones. The result: cloudless skies in the morning.

—beavers build dams?

A beaver's home, called a lodge, is built on an island of mud, stone, and twigs, and to keep out unwanted visitors, it is built with an underwater entrance. If this structure were built in a regular pond, the lodge might be flooded in the rainy season when the water rises and might have its entrance exposed during the dry seasons when the water recedes. To prevent this from happening, beavers build dams downstream of their lodges to keep the water at a constant level.

—girl's short socks are called "bobby socks"?

"Bobby" comes from *bob*, meaning to cut short, as in bobtail and bobby pins—pins used with bobbed hair. Since the socks described by the term are cut much shorter than the earlier knee-length socks girls wore, they were called "bobby socks."

Ever Wonder Why?

—popcorn pops?

Popcorn, a variety of Indian corn called *Zea mays everta*, is different from ordinary corn in that it has a harder outer shell. As the corn is heated, moisture in its starchy grains is converted to steam, causing a tremendous pressure to be exerted against the shell. The tough shell stands up under the pressure for a while but eventually breaks down and the kernel explodes with such force that it throws out its white, pulpy insides, making an audible popping sound in the process.

—car doors open rear to front?

In the days when car door latches weren't as secure as they are today, it was found that doors that swing open front to rear were more likely to be pulled open by air pressure that builds up around a fast-moving car. With doors that open rear to front, the air pressure actually helps prevent the door from coming open.

—one who bluffs is called a "four-flusher"?

In poker a flush is a very good hand consisting of five cards of the same suit. Sometimes a player who has four cards of the same suit showing and a fifth card facedown will pretend that the facedown card is also of the same suit, which would make it a flush. If the facedown card is, in fact, not of the same suit and if the player succeeds in driving the other players out of the game with the bluff, then the player will have won the hand with a four-card flush. A person who does this is called a "four-flusher." In general use the term means one who puts up any sort of bluff.

Ever Wonder Why?

—a dark spot on a woman's face is called a beauty mark?

The idea of the beauty mark began during the smallpox epidemic of the 1600s, which left many European women marred with small scars caused by the disease's blisters. To divert attention from these blemishes, women began wearing small beauty patches on their faces near the eyes or lips. These patches were usually made of black silk and cut in the shape of hearts, stars, or crescents.

After Dr. Edward Jenner found a vaccine for smallpox in 1796, the use of beauty patches decreased, but women continued to decorate their faces with small, pencil marks, which they then called beauty marks. Today almost any dark spot on a woman's face might be called a beauty mark.

—a family's heraldic symbol is called a "coat of arms"?

In medieval Europe men serving under a feudal lord in battle needed some way to identify one another. This was particularly true during the Crusades when many nations fought together. To provide this identification, shields were painted with brightly colored symbols called "arms" that identified the feudal lord. Men of lower rank wore badges showing this same symbol.

Knights usually had this symbol emblazoned on light cloth tunics or coats that they wore over their armor. This tunic became known as a "coat of arms," and later the term came to mean the heraldic symbol itself.

Ever Wonder Why?

—angels are pictured with halos?

Long before the birth of Christ, sun worshipers wore rings of feathers on their heads, presumably to represent rays of sunlight and identify the wearer with the sun god. It is believed that this led to the idea of depicting divine beings with circles of light about their heads. It is also probable that this led kings and queens to wear crowns.

—strips of dried beef are called "beef jerky"?

In the days when the West was being settled, meat was often cut into long, thick strips, dried in the sun, and carried in saddlebags until needed for a meal. The name given to this meat was *charqui*, a Spanish word meaning dried meat. When the meat was beef, the dried strips were called "beef *charqui*," which was later pronounced—and spelled—"beef jerky."

—the names of British firms are often followed by the letters "Ltd"?

"Ltd" stands for "Limited," and it means that the financial liability of the owners of the firm is limited to just the assets they have invested. That is, the owners' personal assets cannot be attached to satisfy claims against the firm. The letters "Inc." following the names of American companies have a similar meaning.

—a necktie tied in a slipknot is called a "four-in-hand" tie?

When a driver of a team of four horses holds all four reins in one hand, he is said to be driving "four-in-hand." A necktie tied in a slipknot falls from its knot in a pattern reminiscent of the reins falling from the hand of a four-in-hand driver. Hence its name.

Ever Wonder Why?

—13 is an unlucky number?

Some attribute this superstition to the Last Supper at which there were thirteen: Christ and the twelve disciples. Though this perception may have strengthened the superstition, the fear of thirteen actually predates the Last Supper. Its origin is found in a part of Norse mythology having to do with a banquet at Valhalla at which Balder, the favorite of the gods, was killed by Loki. Only twelve gods had been invited to the banquet, but Loki, the spirit of discord, intruded, bringing the number to thirteen.

—people tell you to "keep your shirt on" when they want you to calm down?

Not long ago, when men were getting ready to fight, they took off their shirts. "Keep your shirt on" means don't get mad enough to fight.

Ever Wonder Why?

—rainbows are round?

You see a rainbow when the sky in front of you is full of raindrops and the sun is at your back. The parallel rays from the sun pass over your head and strike the raindrops, which act like little prisms. As a ray of light enters the drop, it is broken into its constituent colors red, orange, yellow, green, blue, and violet. Each of these colored rays then strike the back wall of the raindrop and is reflected back toward the front. These reflected, colored rays leave the raindrop at a certain angle, and they can be seen only when they enter the eye at that same angle; just as a small object can be seen in a tiny mirror only when the viewer moves so that the object's reflected image enters the eye at a certain angle. Therefore, in order to see the colored rays reflected out of a single raindrop, the eye, the sun, and the raindrop must be at one specific angle. And to see the reflected rays coming from millions of raindrops, this angle of reflection must be exactly the same for each drop.

Now if you were asked to arrange several million raindrops so that the angle between the sun, the drop, and the viewer's eye was always the same, you would find that you had to arrange the drops in a circle. A circle is the only arrangement that would allow this angle to stay the same. To see this, imagine a cone placed flat-end down in a drinking glass. Note that the angle between the sides of the cone and the sides of the glass remain the same only because the cone is circular. Any change in the shape of the cone would clearly change the angle. In this analogy, the sides of the glass represent the parallel rays of the sun, the bottom rim of the glass represents the field of raindrops, the sides of the cone are the reflected rays of colored light, and the tip of the cone is the viewer's eye.

Ever Wonder Why?

This means that, even though all of the raindrops before you are reflecting the colors of the rainbow, your eye can see only those that are arranged in a circle. And, of course, you can see only the half of the circle that appears above the horizon.

—someone who is feeling great is "on cloud nine"?
Types of clouds are numbered according to the altitudes they attain, with nine being the highest cloud. So if someone is on cloud nine, that person is floating well above worldly cares.

—rice is thrown at weddings?
Since early Roman times some grain—usually wheat—has been associated with the wedding ceremony. Wheat, a symbol of fertility, was carried in the bride's hand or worn by her in the form of a garland. As the bride left the church, grains of wheat were tossed at her, and young girls rushed to pick up the grains that had actually touched the bride. These were assumed to have the power to ensure the young girl a wedding of her own in the near future.

During the reign of Queen Elizabeth I, wheat was no longer tossed at brides but was instead baked into small cakes that were then crumbled and tossed over the bride's head. Later the small cakes were replaced by one large one, which was cooked and eaten.

This change in ceremony left the wedding guests feeling deprived, since they had nothing to toss at the bride. Since at that time rice was cheap, clean, and white, it seemed a good substitute for the more expensive wheat cakes.

Ever Wonder Why?

**—someone not doing his job is said to be
"not worth his salt"?**

At one time soldiers in ancient Rome were paid, in part, with a ration of salt called a salarium, from the Latin word *sal* meaning salt. If a soldier's performance was not up to standard, that soldier was said to be "not worth his salt."

Later, when the salt was replaced with a money allowance to buy the salt, the allowance itself was called a salarium. Eventually, salarium came to mean the wages themselves, and this led to our calling one's pay a salary.

—a book of maps is called an atlas?

Because the earliest books of maps had a picture of Atlas holding the world on his back on the cover.

**—there are often two buttons in the center of
the back of a coat with tails?**

The buttons were there so that the wearer could button up the tails before getting on a horse. Of course, the buttons serve no purpose now.

**—a performer's last work is called his or her
"swan song"?**

This comes from an ancient belief that swans sing beautifully just before they die. Although swans normally make no musical sounds at all, there is evidence that some swans emit unusual musical notes when they are near death.

Ever Wonder Why?

—a groom carries the bride over the threshold?

According to an old superstition, doorways were powerful places where menacing spirits lurked, posing dangers for any stranger entering the house. A man carried his new bride over the threshold to sneak her past these evil spirits. Presumably, these spirits ceased to be as much of a threat once the new wife was no longer a stranger.

—prostitutes are called "hookers"?

During the Civil War a general in charge of the Union Army of the Potomac decided to bolster morale by permitting prostitutes to have access to his troops. The general's name was Joseph "Fighting Joe" Hooker, and the prostitutes who frequented his headquarters became known as "Hooker's girls." Later, when a section of Washington was set aside for brothels, it was called "Hooker's Division," and the prostitutes themselves called "hookers."

—some animals' eyes seem to glow in the dark?

Nocturnal animals can see well at night partly because of a white compound called guanine in the retina. This substance provides a mirrorlike surface that reflects incoming light back toward the front, giving the animal's eyes a second chance to absorb light images. This reflected light is what makes an animal's eyes appear to glow in the dark.

Ever Wonder Why?

—purple is considered a royal color?

The first purple dye, known to the Romans as purpura, was made from small cysts on a species of Mediterranean shellfish. Each shellfish yielded only a tiny amount of the substance needed to make the dye, so the dye itself was very rare and very expensive. Since it was affordable only by the very rich, it became a symbol of high rank.

—dull students are called dunces?

Dunces are named after John Duns Scotus, a thirteenth-century theologian and philosopher. Scotus's writings were required reading in universities for about two centuries after his death, but by the sixteenth century his followers were viewed as sophists who wouldn't face up to issues and who tried to confuse matters with clever arguments. They were called Dunsmen by their critics, and the word *duns* came to mean a hairsplitter. Some time between then and now duns became dunce and the term came to mean a stupid person.

—swiss cheese has holes?

Swiss cheese is made by heating cow's milk at high temperatures and then lifting the curd from the whey in one mass in a fine-mesh net. This mass is then shaped into blocks, salted with strong brine, wrapped to prevent drying, and stored for six to eight weeks to ferment at 80° Fahrenheit. The holes are formed during this latter part of the process when bubbles of carbon dioxide gas are liberated by bacteria used to promote fermentation.

Ever Wonder Why?

—gasoline trucks carry those metal chains that drag the ground?

As a truck rolls along the highway, it is possible for a large charge of static electricity to build up on the surface of the truck as a result of the interaction of the truck's tires and the pavement. There is a possibility that this much electric charge could, under the right conditions, cause a spark and ignite the gasoline. By dragging the chain along the ground, any built-up charge will flow harmlessly down the chain to the ground.

Not everyone agrees that the chain offers this much protection, but that is why it is there.

—someone thoroughly drunk is described as being "three sheets to the wind"?

The "sheets" referred to are control ropes attached to the sails on a ship. When three of these sheets are untied and allowed to run free, the uncontrolled sails flap in the wind and the ship lurches and staggers like a drunk person. Therefore a person acting this way is said to be "three sheets to the wind."

—a man's coat comes with those useless buttons on the sleeves?

Buttons were first put on sleeves during a time when men preferred their sleeves to fit very tightly. The buttons were put there so that the man could unbutton the sleeves to get his hands through.

Ever Wonder Why?

—the notes taken at a meeting are called "minutes"?

The word *minute* as it is used here is actually the word *minute*, with the accent on the second syllable. Long ago, notes taken at a meeting were first written in a very small (or minute) hand and then later transcribed to a larger hand. The small notes themselves were called minutes, and at that time minute, meaning small, was pronounced exactly the same as minute, meaning a unit of time.

—ostriches put their heads in the ground?

Ostriches rarely put their heads in the ground, but when they do, they are just looking for water below the surface.

—using someone else's ideas without giving credit is called "stealing that person's thunder"?

In 1709 an English playwright named John Dennis produced a play called *Appius and Virginia*, which opened at Drury Lane in London. For the play's sound effects Dennis had developed a new way of simulating the sound of thunder using wooden troughs. The thunder was a success, but Dennis's play was a failure, and the people at Drury Lane soon closed it.

A bit later Dennis went to Drury Lane to see a performance of *Macbeth* and was enraged to discover that his new technique of making thunder was being used. He was quoted as saying, "That's my thunder, by God! The villains will not play my play, but they steal my thunder!" This gave rise to the expression.

Ever Wonder Why?

**——it is customary for the father of the bride
to pay for the wedding?**

At one time a man literally purchased his wife from her family. As a gift to the husband, and to offset this expense, it became customary for the wife's family to present the husband with a dowry. The current practice of the bride's father paying for the wedding is an outgrowth of the idea behind the dowry; that is, something contributed by the bride's family to the groom.

——a football playing field is called a "gridiron"?

Because it looks like one. A gridiron, of course, is a flat framework of parallel bars used for cooking meat or fish. Viewed from above, the markings on a football field resemble a gridiron.

**——a person who is very angry is said to be
"seeing red"?**

Extreme anger can really make a person see red. Under certain conditions a state of rage can cause the eyes to become suffused with blood, causing the person to see things through a reddish haze.

However, this expression most likely comes from a comparison to the anger a bull shows when the matador shakes a red cape in front of it.

Ever Wonder Why?

—the devil is portrayed as having horns
and hooved feet?

This image of the devil began with medieval art, and it is believed to have been taken from the descriptions of satyrs in Greek mythology. The satyrs were attendants of Bacchus, the god of wine, and they were characterized as lazy, lecherous, evil drunkards who spent much of their time chasing nymphs through the forests. The satyrs had small horns and hooved feet.

—a sports enthusiast is called a "fan"?

"Fan" is an abbreviation for fanatic. Toward the turn of the century the media referred to football enthusiasts first as football fanatics and then later as football fans.

—severe and prolonged questioning is called the
"third degree"?

In Freemasonry the third degree is the highest degree attainable, that of Master Mason. For a long time people believed that in order to qualify for this degree a mason had to undergo a series of severe, proficiency tests. The tests are really quite simple, but because of this belief the term "third degree" came to mean any severe interrogation.

—a room where guests are received and entertained
is sometimes called a drawing room?

The room was originally called a "withdrawing room," since it was the one to which guests would withdraw after dinner. Over time it was simply abbreviated to "drawing room."

Ever Wonder Why?

—it was once believed by some that handling a toad can give one warts?

Because toads look as if they are covered with warts, some people believed that warts could be "caught" by simply touching a toad. Of course, this is not true.

—money set aside for corrupt purposes is called a "slush fund"?

"Slush" refers to refuse fat and grease from a cook's galley. In the British navy many years ago a ship's slush was often sold as a lubricant, with the proceeds being used to buy small luxuries for the ship's enlisted men. The money resulting from these sales was called the ship's "slush fund."

Later the term was applied to a fund set up for similar purposes but contributed to by the enlisted men. Today, of course, the term refers to money to be used for bribery, political payoffs, or other corrupt practices.

—those little red schoolhouses were red?

Because red paint was cheap. In New England in the 1800s a homemade paint containing iron oxide was very popular because it acted as an excellent wood preservative. It was used on wooden barns, sheds, stores, and schoolhouses.

It gave the structures a hard, protective coat, and because of the iron oxide, it also gave them a bright red color.

Ever Wonder Why?

—toll roads are called "turnpikes"?

The word *turnpike* comes from an older word *turnpyke*, meaning a rotating barrier with pikes (spikes) used to control entrance to a toll road. Roads protected in this manner were called turnpikes. Even after less severe means—such as toll booths and turnstiles—were used to control access, the name turnpike was still used.

—S.O.S. is used as the universal distress call?

Because the Morse code for these letters is easy to remember: 3 dashes—3 dots—3 dashes. The letters themselves do not stand for anything.

—when people don't understand something, they say "It's Greek to me"?

This expression comes from the first act of Shakespeare's *Julius Caesar*. It was spoken by Casca who was describing words he had heard Cicero use regarding Caesar's refusal to accept the crown of emperor. Cicero was, in fact, speaking in Greek to prevent an eavesdropper from understanding what he said. The expression caught on as a way of showing confusion about something that was said.

—naval academy students are called "midshipmen"?

In the British navy two centuries ago young naval officers being trained aboardship were usually assigned quarters on the lower deck near the middle of the ship. For this reason they were called "midshipmen."

The naval academy at Annapolis copied the British and applied the term to their own naval officers in training.

Ever Wonder Why?

—the dead are buried aboveground in New Orleans?

New Orleans is built on lowlands formed from silt deposited by the Mississippi River. As a result the subsoil in New Orleans has, in the past, been too damp for belowground burials. The dead, therefore, were buried in aboveground vaults or tombs.

—we say something is as "dead as a doornail"?

Some say the doornail in question is the large knob that a metal door knocker strikes and that it is dead as a result of the continuous pounding it takes.

Others say the doornail is a large-headed nail used in the construction of the door. This nail is also pounded very hard so that the head is flattened, giving the nail a firmer grip in the wood.

Pianos have black and white keys?

The white keys, of course, are the result of a decision made long ago to cover the regular keys on the piano with ivory. Ivory was chosen because of its beauty, its durability, and its high susceptibility to polish.

When it came to constructing the remaining keys—the sharps and the flats—it was decided that these should be made from a substance very close to ivory in feel and appearance and as visually distinguishable from the white keys as possible. It was found that these requirements could be met by ebony wood. It is hard, heavy, very durable, easily polished, and as black as pitch. Ebony, therefore, became the choice for the sharp and flat keys.

Ever Wonder Why?

—monkeys in the zoo spend so much time preening the hair of other monkeys?

Monkeys in the wild do this because they are looking for body parasites, but monkeys in the zoo are relatively free of such parasites. What the monkeys in the zoo are looking for are bits of salt that have exuded through the pores of the monkey's skin and have dried out under the hair.

—some Londoners are called cockneys?

The word *cockney* comes from two Middle English words, "coken ey," which means cock's egg. It refers to small, misshapened, yolkless hen eggs that were once believed to be laid by cocks. At various times the term has been used to describe spoiled children, sissies, effeminate men, and especially city slickers. Since in the seventeenth century London was the major city, the term was applied specifically to Londoners and was, by this time, pronounced "cockney." Its meaning has since been narrowed further, so that today it applies chiefly to Londoners from the East End.

—blue means obscene, as in "blue movies"?

The association of the word *blue* with obscenity originated with a series of risqué French books called *La Bibliothèque Bleu*, or the blue library.

—a pair of aces and a pair of jacks in poker is called a dead man's hand?

Because this is the hand Wild Bill Hickok was holding when he was accused of cheating and shot dead by Jack McCall in Deadwood, South Dakota, in 1876.

Ever Wonder Why?

—something flimsily built is said to be "jerry built"?

The French word for day is *jour*, and this word was once used to describe something built to last only a short time. For instance, a jour-mast was a makeshift wooden mast intended to last only until a proper one could be constructed. Jour-mast was soon mispronounced as jury-mast and then as jerry-mast, with the spelling of the term suffering as well. This usage eventually led to the general term "jerry built," which, if taken literally, means built to last one day.

—races have first, second, and third prizes?

This practice is the result of a silversmith's inability to satisfy his customer.

In the early seventeenth century in Chester, England, the sheriff agreed to provide a silver trophy for a horse race and contracted with a silversmith to do the work. The silversmith's first trophy was unacceptable, and he was sent back for another try. The second one, too, was unsatisfactory, and he was instructed to try a third time. The third trophy was fine, but now the sheriff had three trophies instead of one. So as not to be wasteful the sheriff decided to award trophies to the first, second, and third place winners.

—something deliberately misleading is called a red herring?

In the seventeenth century criminals fleeing from the law found that they could throw the police's bloodhounds off the scent by dragging a piece of cured, strong-smelling red herring across their trail. Hence the expression.

Ever Wonder Why?

—people say "Roger" to indicate they understand?

In Morse code the letter *R* was used to indicate "understood," and when voice communication became popular, *R* kept this meaning. In voice systems words—such as *Able, Baker, Charlie*—were assigned to letters to lessen the chance of misunderstanding, and *Roger* was the word assigned to the letter *R*. Therefore, "Roger" came to mean "I understand."

—the men who assist a fighter in a boxing match are called seconds?

In early boxing matches each boxer was allowed to have two assistants in his corner. Usually these assistants were boxers themselves and were there to engage in a second boxing match or to participate in a substitute match if the first one ended too quickly. Because they were involved in second matches, they were called "seconds."

—a face is called a mug?

Two hundred years ago it was common practice to design drinking mugs to look like ugly faces. It wasn't long before someone made the reverse association and began referring to faces, perhaps ugly ones, as mugs.

—the size of nails is measured in pennies?

Nails in England were once sold by the hundreds. Nails that sold for ten pence per hundred were known as 10-penny nails, larger nails that sold for twenty pence were called 20-penny nails, and so on. Though the pricing has long since changed, we still use the penny designation to specify the size of a nail.

Ever Wonder Why?

—marines are called "leathernecks"?

Sailors gave the marines this name because of a stiff, leather-collar lining marines once wore to make their collars stand up in military fashion. The leather lining, however, proved to be a bad idea because of the problems it caused when it got wet with perspiration. It was done away with around 1875.

—a practice based upon general experience is called a "rule of thumb"?

The thumb has been used frequently as a means of making approximate measurements. Clothiers and carpenters used it to measure one inch, and cooks and brewers used it to test the temperature of heated liquids. Measurements made this way were said to be made according to the "rule of thumb." In general use the expression has been expanded to include any method or procedure based on practice or experience rather than on scientific knowledge.

—we say that something fits "to a T"?

Apparently, something that fits to a T fits as well as if it had been constructed using an engineer's T-square.

—we say that someone who is ill-tempered must have "gotten up on the wrong side of the bed"?

The saying means that the person must have gotten up on the left side of the bed. Left has long been associated with bad things. For instance, the word *sinister* comes from the Latin word meaning left and the word *gauche* comes from the French word for left. So if someone is grumpy, perhaps it is because he or she got up on the left, or wrong, side of the bed.

Ever Wonder Why?

—we talk about making money "hand over fist"?

Picture the hands of a fisherman as he hauls in a large net full of fish. First one fist holds the rope while the other hand moves over it to get a new grip farther down. Then that fist holds the rope while the first hand moves over it to get a new grip—and so on "hand over fist." Now picture the net full of money, and you will see how the above expression came about.

—"toe the line" means to follow orders strictly?

The line in the expression refers to one drawn across the center of a boxing ring many years ago. At the beginning of each round the boxers were required to "toe the line," that is, touch the line with their toes. If a boxer was unable to comply with this rule within eight seconds, he lost the bout.

—arousing someone's interest is said to be "getting a rise out of him"?

This was originally a fly fisherman's term describing the way fish rise to bait cast upon the surface of the water. Used figuratively, it means getting anyone to "rise to the bait."

—we say "what the Dickens"?

"Dickens" in this usage is possibly a corruption of the word *devilkins*, which means little devils. If so, the phrase really means "what the devil."

Ever Wonder Why?

—so many pencils are yellow?

Pencils painted yellow were sold as early as 1854, but yellow didn't become the predominant color for pencils until around 1890. It was at that time that the L&C Hardtmuth Company of Austria introduced a pencil of such high quality that it became the standard for others to follow. The pencil was named Koh-I-Noor after the famous Indian diamond, and it was painted golden yellow, supposedly because, with its black lead, that made it the color of the Austro-Hungarian flag. This pencil, which was advertised as "the original yellow pencil," was such a huge success that it established yellow as the symbol of quality in pencils. Other pencil manufacturers soon began painting their pencils yellow, and today three out of four pencils sold are that color.

—some animals sleep through winter?

Animals sleep through the winter because there is so little food available in the winter that they would starve if they were active. Nature has designed things so that these animals can eat enough extra food just before winter to meet their bodies' needs at the lower metabolic rate during their winter sleep.

Ever Wonder Why?

—it is okay to kiss someone under mistletoe?

For centuries many of our forebears believed that mistletoe had special powers, probably because mistletoe seemed to appear magically in the upper branches of trees. The Druids believed that the plant was sacred, and other ancient Britons thought it could cure sterility and act as an antidote for poisons.

The Romans made mistletoe a part of their Saturnalia, an ancient feast in honor of the god Saturn held around December 17 to celebrate the winter solstice and the completion of the year's agricultural work. During this festival there was feasting, unrestrained revelry, and a temporary disregard for all rules of conduct. Enemies were treated as friends, slaves were served by their masters, and all lines of propriety were ignored. The attitude during the Saturnalia was "anything goes," and this came to be symbolized by the mistletoe.

When the Christians began using mistletoe to decorate their churches during the Christmas season, some of its Saturnalian reputation caused problems. Among other things, it emboldened young men to steal kisses from young ladies when they were near mistletoe. Eventually it was banned from the sanctuary, but it then moved to the halls and chambers in other parts of the church where it continued to cast its charms.

Ever Wonder Why?

—something genuine is called "the real McCoy"?

The real McCoy was most probably Kid McCoy, the world welterweight boxing champion from 1890 to 1900. The Kid was such a popular fighter that other, less well-known fighters traveling the small-town boxing circuit claimed to be Kid McCoy to draw crowds and increase the size of the gate. The problem of imitators became so severe that McCoy began billing himself as Kid "The Real" McCoy, and from this came the expression we now apply to any genuine article.

—floral wreaths are placed on graves?

The placing of the wreath is what remains of an ancient belief that it was necessary to provide comforts for the dead and give them gifts so that their spirits would not haunt the mourners. The circular arrangement represents a magic circle that is supposed to keep the spirit within its bounds.

—a bride always stands on the groom's left?

In the days when men often captured their brides from neighboring villages, a groom had to stay alert to the possibility of an attack by the bride's kinsmen or by jealous suitors. This made it necessary for the bridegroom to keep his right hand free during the ceremony to fend off any such attacks. This, of course, meant that the bride had to stand on his left.

Ever Wonder Why?

**——having an ulterior motive is sometimes
referred to as "having an ax to grind"?**

A writer and publisher named Charles Miner gave birth
to this expression in a story that appeared in his publication,
The Gleaner and Luzerne Intelligencer, in 1811. The story
describes an occurrence in Miner's youth when he was
approached by a very cordial man carrying an ax. After
winning young Miner over with praise and flattery, the
man talked him into sharpening the ax on a grindstone in
the family's yard. Miner did a fine job of sharpening the
ax but received no thanks from the man who had been so
friendly just moments before. From this experience Miner
concluded, "When I see a merchant over-polite to his customers, begging them to taste a little brandy and throwing
half his goods on the counter—thinks I, that man has an ax
to grind."

**——in the animal kingdom, the male is often
prettier than the female?**

Since, in the animal kingdom, it is often the female of
the species that selects the mate, the male is the one that
has to be attractive. Females tend to prefer males with the
most striking coloration and features, so the males tend to
be prettier—especially during the breeding season.

While it is necessary for the male to be striking for the
above reason, it is also very dangerous, since predators are
more likely to spot a brightly colored animal than a dull
one. Thus the female's duller color provides her with some
protection.

Ever Wonder Why?

—an unbelievable story is called a "cock and bull" story?

This is believed to be derived from ancient fables in which preposterous situations were acted out by talking animals—such as cocks and bulls.

—the color green is associated with envy?

A greenish facial tint has long been associated with illness, as suggested by the expression "green around the gills." Since a person who is deeply envious is considered by many to be unwell, such persons are described as "green (sick) with envy."

—a drink given to one just recovering from a drinking binge is called the "hair of the dog that bit you"?

Ancient cures often called for a second dose of the very thing that caused a problem in the first place. This theory of treatment was known as *similia similibus curantar*, meaning "like cures like." In particular, if one was bitten by a dog, the remedy involved placing some of the dog's hair (often charred) on the wound. A similar treatment for a hangover required that the sufferer have another drink of the same liquor the next morning. The two ideas were combined and the second drink of liquor was called the "hair of the dog that bit you."

Ever Wonder Why?

—we knock on wood for good luck?

The good luck associated with wood probably comes from pagan times when trees were worshiped and believed to contain the spirits of gods. For instance, since lightning so often strikes trees, the oak was believed by some ancient cultures to be the dwelling place of the god of lightning and thunder. To touch a tree or rap on it was a means of summoning the spirits within to come forth and provide the person doing the rapping with protection from evil.

—golf courses are called golf "links"?

The word *links* comes from an Anglo-Saxon word *hlinc* meaning slope. Since the earliest golf courses were situated on grassy slopes—that is, gentle rolling land—they were called golf "links."

—one who fails at something is said to have "laid an egg"?

The egg, in this case, is actually a zero score, which is sometimes called a goose egg or duck egg. The phrase was used as early as 1863 to describe a player who had failed to score any points in a cricket match. With time the phrase came to mean almost any sort of failure.

Ever Wonder Why?

—birds sing?

Male birds do most of the singing, and they do it to stake out their territory and to invite the female of the species to mate.

It is interesting that females tend to select as mates those male birds that sing the most. The females do this, it is believed, not because they like the singing but because they have learned that the males that sing the most have the most food in their territory. Since the male doesn't have to spend much time hunting for food, it has more time to sing. Thus the females tend to chose these mates not because of how well they sing but because they are rich.

—you must not put metal cookware into a microwave oven?

First, because the metal would reflect the microwaves and keep them from penetrating the food. Second, because the metal could cause arcing to occur inside the oven. Arcing is similar to lightning and can damage the oven.

Ever Wonder Why?

—annoying someone is called "getting his goat"?

For reasons that are unclear, horses form unusually close attachments to goats. The presence of a goat can have a calming effect on a horse, and this fact has been used by horse trainers in the past to calm high-strung animals. Once quieted in this manner, a horse becomes very agitated if the goat is taken away. It has been suggested that this is the reason we describe annoying someone as getting his goat.

—zebras have stripes?

The stripes camouflage the zebra and help it hide from its enemies. They do this by breaking up the outline of the zebra when it moves through tall grass. Instead of getting a clear view of the zebra, all a predator sees is a bunch of vertical lines. This is particularly true on a hot day when hazy heat waves are rising from the earth.

Ever Wonder Why?

—the English drive on the left and we drive on the right?

This custom, it seems, resulted from the difference in the way large horse-drawn, or oxen-drawn, wagons were once designed here and in England. In this country such wagons were usually designed without a seat for the driver. The Conestoga wagon, or "prairie schooner," is an example of this type of wagon. The driver either walked along the left side of the wagon or rode on the animal in the left rear position. Being on the left was necessary in order for a right-handed driver to crack a whip over the animals' backs. When driver and team encountered another driver and team coming from the opposite direction, the positions of the two drivers made it natural for them to move their teams to the right. Moving to the right was also necessary in order for the drivers to keep an eye on the inside wheels to make sure they passed without colliding. This was so important that, in 1792, a law was passed in Pennsylvania requiring that wagons pass each other by moving to the right.

In England the large wagons were built differently, with a driver seat in the front. To control a team of animals, a driver of this type of wagon found it necessary to sit on the right side so that the brake lever, which was on the right, could be manipulated. This position made it natural for the driver to pull the team to the left when passing an oncoming wagon, again to allow both drivers to keep an eye on the inside wheels.

With the wagons in America keeping to the right and those in England keeping to the left, it was not surprising that when horseless carriages came into being, they followed the same custom.

Ever Wonder Why?

—a presentation is sometimes called a "dog and pony show"?

"Dog and pony show" originally described—somewhat sarcastically—a small circus that had little to offer in the way of animal acts. No lions, no elephants, no horses—just dogs and ponies. After a while the expression was used to describe any unimpressive performance.

—we yawn?

It is believed that the yawn, by causing the lungs to take in a larger than normal volume of air and by stretching the face muscles, helps the body keep from falling asleep.

—a Caesar salad goes by that name?

Caesar Gardini of Tijuana, Mexico, is the man responsible for the name of this famous salad. The salad itself was a spur-of-the-moment concoction, invented by Gardini to serve an unexpected influx of tourists one day in his restaurant, Caesar's Place. Using ingredients on hand, Gardini served the tourists salads consisting of romaine lettuce, grated cheese, croutons, and anchovies with a dressing made from olive oil, lemon juice, garlic, and coddled eggs. The invention was a success, and when the salad was duplicated in other restaurants, it was called Caesar's salad.

—one who crosses a street illegally is called a jaywalker?

The word *jay*, as it is used here, means a rustic and not-too-smart person who is probably in the big city for the first time. The term "jaywalker" describes someone who crosses city streets in a dangerous manner as a jay might.

Ever Wonder Why?

—the lights on police cars are now often blue instead of red?

The blue lights are to clearly differentiate police cars from other emergency vehicles, thereby correcting a long-standing problem.

It used to be that drivers who decided to flee from the police could later claim that they thought the red light behind them belonged to some other emergency vehicle. That meant that they could be charged only with failing to yield to an emergency vehicle. To avoid confusion and remove this as a possible alibi, the lights on police cars were changed to a different color.

Blue was chosen because of its excellent visibility and uniqueness.

—you blink your eyes?

You blink your eyes to keep them clean. Each time the eyelid moves over the surface of the eye, it spreads a layer of water that clears the surface of small debris.

—tombstones are placed at grave sites?

In very early times tombstones were laid on top of graves to weigh down the soil and keep the spirit in the grave from getting out. Later, when the stone was erected upright, it was used to mark the grave so that an unsuspecting stroller would not walk on the grave and become defiled by the spirit within, which at that time was believed to be impure.

Ever Wonder Why?

—$ means dollars?

In the late eighteenth century the American colonies wanted their basic unit of currency to be as different as possible from the British pound. In 1782 Thomas Jefferson declared that the basic unit of currency would be the Spanish dollar or peso. The peso was already in wide use and, according to Jefferson, was "a known coin and most familiar to the minds of the people."

This coin had engraved on its obverse side two pillars representing the Pillars of Hercules at Gibraltar and was called the "pillar dollar." In writing it was symbolized by two vertical lines with an *S* over the top of them to indicate plural. That is, $, the sign we have adopted for the American dollar.

—auctioneers call out bids in that peculiar, singsong manner?

An auctioneer's rapid chant is designed to provide order to the bidding process and keep the bids coming in rapid succession. There is a great deal of uncertainty and hesitation among bidders at a large auction, and this chant acts as a steady cadence that urges the bidders to place their bids quickly. To control a very rapid bidding process auctioneers had to develop an almost musical chant as the only means of enunciating the bids fast enough to keep up the pace.

The chant is made to sound even more peculiar by the odd filler phrases auctioneers use to maintain the tempo of the auction. One such filler is "Give me the bid. Little bit more," which comes out sounding like "gimmedebid libbydemo." All of this may make the auctioneers sound funny, but it is essential to the smooth operation of the auction.

Ever Wonder Why?

—hair turns gray?

The color of hair is due to a pigment called melanin, and the lightness or darkness of hair is determined by the amount of melanin it contains. When people get older, the body usually stops producing this pigment, leaving the hair without color—that is, leaving it gray or white.

—ice on the back of the neck can sometimes stop or slow a nosebleed?

The ice reduces the temperature in the area of the neck containing the blood vessels carrying blood to the nose. This causes the vessels to contract and close up, thus stopping or slowing the flow of blood.

—the steering wheel on a powerboat is normally on the right-hand side?

The rules of the nautical road require that powerboats yield to other vessels approaching from their right. To give the skipper of such a boat a clear view in this direction, steering wheels are traditionally placed on the right-hand side of the boat.

Ever Wonder Why?

—rubber tires won't stay buried?

Most people, having never tried to bury a tire, are not aware that one will not stay in the ground. In fact, if you bury a tire five feet below the surface, it will—under normal conditions—rise to the top in about ten years.

The reason for this is as follows. The rubber tire, being resilient, is constantly pushing back against the soil around it. And since the pressure above the tire is less than that below it, the tire has more success pushing up than it does pushing down. As this pushing proceeds, small particles of soil around the tire are dislodged and fall down through cracks and crevices too small for the tire itself to fit through, a process that is accelerated somewhat by the slight movement of the tire as it expands and contracts with changes in temperature. Thus, as the tire pushes upward and the soil around it slowly moves down, the tire migrates toward the surface.

—opossums sleep hanging upside down by their tails?

The opossum's tail is, of course, prehensile, meaning that it is well adapted to grasping and holding on to things. And the opossum uses its tail in just that way. It holds on to tree limbs to keep from falling, holds on to its young to keep them from falling, and it sometimes even hangs by its tail—and one or more of its paws—when it is eating, grooming its young, or reaching for something it could not reach in any other way. But the fact is, opossums do not sleep hanging upside down by their tails, and drawings of them doing this are inaccurate. Opossums sleep on top of limbs, in crevices, or in recesses just like most other arboreal animals.

Ever Wonder Why?

—the army requires its recruits to have such short haircuts?

Short haircuts became a strict military tradition only after campaigns were fought in tropical climates where the danger of scalp infestation was greatly increased. This, coupled with a general advance in medicine at that time, led the army to require its field soldiers to cut their hair very close to the scalp. This was done to make the scalp easier to clean, to make scalp wounds easier to treat, and to make the hair less trouble to care for under battle conditions.

—a crescent moon is carved into so many of the outhouses you see in pictures?

When outhouses were in wide use, many people were unable to read, so men's and women's outhouses had to be identified with symbols. The crescent moon, symbolizing Luna, the moon goddess of Roman mythology, had become a universal symbol of womankind, so it was used to identify the ladies' outhouse. The sunburst, symbol of Sol, the sun god, was used on the men's outhouses. With time, the men's outhouses fell into disuse and were soon abandoned. Apparently, men found ways to get along without enclosed facilities. The ladies' outhouses, however, were better maintained and lasted longer. And that is why you see the crescent moon on so many outhouses shown in pictures today.

Ever Wonder Why?

—the sea is salty?

Some of the salt in the ocean comes from underwater volcanos, but the majority of it comes from the erosion of the earth's crust. Mineral salts contained in eroded products are dissolved in rainwater and carried by the earth's rivers to the sea. As the sun evaporates seawater, the salt that was in the water remains behind, increasing the sea's overall saltiness. Today, the sea is about 3.5 percent dissolved mineral salts, with the most common being sodium chloride, or plain old table salt.

—we don't eat horse meat?

For a long time the horse played a central role in pagan religious ceremonies and was frequently slaughtered in sacrifice to a pagan god. In certain sects the ritual also included eating the flesh of the slaughtered animal and drinking its blood in the belief that so doing would impart some of the horse's strength and speed to the worshiper.

The Christians viewed such pagan rituals as evil and in A.D. 732 Pope Gregory III forbade the eating of horse flesh as a matter of papal law.

Thus, eating horse meat is taboo, not because it is bad for you, but because of its association with ancient pagan rituals.

Ever Wonder Why?

—playing cards are made up of hearts, spades, clubs, and diamonds?

Although playing cards originated in China many centuries ago, in their present form they go back only to fourteenth-century France. It has been suggested that the four standard suits represent the four major classes of fourteenth-century French society. Hearts (shaped like a shield) represent the nobility and the church, spades (shaped like a spear tip) represent the military, clubs (shaped like clover) represent the rural peasant, and diamonds (shaped like the tiles associated with merchants' shops) represent the middle class.

—so many military uniforms are colored khaki?

Khaki uniforms were introduced in 1857 in India at the time of a general uprising of native troops against the British rulers. The British soldiers, finding that their white uniforms made them too good a target for native snipers, attempted to camouflage them with mud and dust to make them blend in better with the dusty, desert background. A British officer picked up on the idea and commissioned a cloth manufacturer to make dust-colored uniforms. The color is called "khaki" after the Hindustani word for "dust-colored."

Ever Wonder Why?

—camels have humps?

The humps are there to store fat. In the way that most animals store fat around their bellies, camels store it in the one or two humps on their backs. When camels cannot get to food, they live off the fat stored in their humps. As the fat is used up, the hump shrinks, and in the case of the two-humped Bactrian camel the tops of the humps flop over to one side. The humps resume their full shape after the camel eats again.

In addition to serving as food storage bins, the fatty humps also insulate the camel from the hot rays of the sun.

—extorted money is called "blackmail"?

When the English owned much of the farmland in Scotland, they charged the Scottish farmers rent called "mail" from a Scottish word meaning rent or taxes. Payments were normally made in silver, and this was called "white mail." When a farmer couldn't raise the silver, the payment had to be made in produce, and this was called "black mail." On the threat of eviction, some landlords demanded much more produce than was actually needed to cover the rent, and this gave the term "blackmail" its present negative connotation.

—doing something thoroughly or all the way is said to be "going whole hog"?

One definition of "hog" is a young sheep not yet shorn. Long ago many farmers chose not to shear hogs completely because the fleece was very short and hard to get to. Others, of a different mind, chose to "go whole hog" and shear the entire sheep. According to popular theory, this is where we got the expression.

Ever Wonder Why?

—a horse race over an obstacle course is called a steeplechase?

In the eighteenth century a group of luckless fox hunters were returning from an unproductive hunt when one of them, deciding that the day should not be a total loss, suggested an interesting race. He bet that he could ride straight to a steeple visible in the distance and touch it with his whip before any of the others. It was agreed that the course to the steeple had to be straight, though, meaning that the riders had to jump obstacles encountered along the way. The bet was accepted, and the first steeplechase began. Later the term was used to describe overland races between several steeples, and now it just means an obstacle course.

—cats are so attracted to catnip?

Catnip contains a substance called nepetalactone that comes from small glands on the leaves of a plant of the mint family called catnip. It is believed that when nepetalactone is inhaled by cats, it alters their brain functioning and arouses sexual feelings, as would a hormone. This causes cats to act playful and exhibit mating-type behavior. So cats are attracted to catnip for the same reason they are attracted to cats of the opposite sex.

Ever Wonder Why?

——most pencils are hexagonal in shape?

Square pencils would be easy to manufacture but not very comfortable to hold; round pencils are comfortable to hold but more costly to manufacture. Hexagonal pencils are a compromise. They are about as comfortable as round pencils yet less costly to make. Nine hexagonal pencils can be produced from the same amount of wood it would take to make eight round ones, and the hexagonal pencils require one less processing step. Hence, the prevalence of hexagonal pencils.

In fact, sales now indicate that the hexagonal shape is preferred eleven to one over the round, perhaps because the hexagonal pencil is less likely to roll off a desk or drawing table.

——we say, "Don't take any wooden nickels"?

This saying goes back to 1915 and probably began simply as a humorous warning to country folk going to the city not to be taken in by city slickers trying to pay them off with wooden nickels. Wooden nickels have never been counterfeited, but wooden coins have often been made as souvenirs of centennials. Perhaps the person who coined this expression had coins such as these in mind.

——so many weather vanes are topped with the figure of a rooster?

In the middle of the ninth century the pope declared that every church steeple should display the image of a cock (or rooster). This cock was to symbolize St. Peter's denial of Christ three times before the cock crowed twice, as discussed in Mark 14:30. Since church steeples were already adorned with weather vanes, the cock was placed on top of these, thereby establishing the trend.

111

Ever Wonder Why?

—we don't see more bodies of small animals such as birds and squirrels that have died of old age or illness?

When an animal feels bad because it is ill or near death, it doesn't carry on with its normal routine while waiting to die on the spot. Instead, it goes to some hideaway, such as a nest, a hole in a tree, or a clump of undergrowth, to protect itself from predators during its weakened condition. Should the animal die, it dies there rather than out in the open, and that is why you don't see dead bodies lying all about. Of course, the bodies soon decompose or are eaten by scavengers.

—someone rescued from a difficult situation at the last minute has been "saved by the bell"?

Contrary to what many believe, this expression did not come from the world of boxing, where a downed fighter can, indeed, be saved by the bell. It originated, instead, in the seventeenth century when a sentry at Windsor Castle was accused of being asleep on duty and was sentenced to death. The sentry denied the charge and offered as proof of his innocence the fact that he had heard the bell in the clock tower of St. Paul's Cathedral strike thirteen times at midnight. At first no one believed that the clock's bell could have been heard from so far away, but then it was discovered that the clock had, in fact, struck thirteen times at midnight on the very night the sentry was supposed to have fallen asleep on duty. The sentry was, of course, released, having been "saved by the bell."

Ever Wonder Why?

—a white flag is used as a signal of truce?

Because it symbolizes untouched purity, the color white has long been used in religious ceremonies all over the world as a sign of innocence and goodwill. Because of this image, white has now become almost universally acknowledged as a sign of peace and is, therefore, a natural choice for a flag of truce.

—the hands on wristwatches in advertisements usually show the time as about 10:10?

This particular arrangement of the hands is used because it nicely frames the name of the watch, which is usually in the upper half of the face, because it doesn't cover any writing in the lower half of the face, and because it is pleasingly symmetrical.

—we drink a toast?

The early Romans began the custom of putting a piece of burned toast into wine to reduce the wine's acidity and improve its flavor, but it wasn't until the eighteenth century that the idea of drinking the toast itself came about. The idea supposedly arose out of an account by Richard Steele that appeared in *The Tatler* in Bath, England, in 1709. As the story goes, two young men who came upon a girl in a public bath were so taken with her beauty that one of them dipped a glass into the bath and drank to her charms. The other said, "Tho I like not the liquor, I will have the toast."

Ever Wonder Why?

—traffic lights are red, yellow, and green?

The first traffic light was invented around 1912 by Lester Farnsworth Wire, who was then head of the traffic division of the Salt Lake City Police Department. His light contained only two lamps, one red and one green. These were colors he took from lights then in use on seagoing vessels and railroad signals where they meant stop and go as they do now.

Red has often been the color chosen when the goal was to attract attention, since red, more than any other color, heightens nervous tension in people. Green, on the other hand, has a neutral effect on human emotions, so it was natural to use it to indicate an "okay to proceed" condition.

When it was decided to add a caution lamp to the traffic light, yellow was chosen because, other than white, it was the color most distinguishable from red and green. White, of course, was not desired since it could be confused with the many other white lights—such as streetlights—that might be near the traffic light.

Ever Wonder Why?

—guarantees are sometimes backed with a promise to "eat one's hat"?

Eggs, dates, salt, saffron, and veal are the main ingredients in an old and terrible-tasting dish that went by the name of "hattes." When someone wanted to give absolute assurance that the agreement would be carried through, he or she would often promise to do so or "eat hattes." Somewhere along the line the word *hattes* was misinterpreted and people began promising to eat their "hats.

—the Chinese eat with chopsticks?

According to one account, a Chinese emperor once so feared a public uprising that he ordered his troops to collect all metal implements that might be used as weapons against him. This, of course, included the metal eating utensils then in use by the Chinese people. Deprived of their knives and forks, the Chinese people, it is said, learned to eat with narrow sticks they cut from bamboo trees, thus giving birth to chopsticks.

Ever Wonder Why?

—there are eighteen holes on a golf course?

The number of holes on golf courses has varied greatly over the past several centuries from five or six to over twenty, but the number eighteen is due to the number of holes eventually decided upon in the mid-eighteenth century by the St. Andrews Society of Golfers in St. Andrews, Scotland (now known as the Royal and Ancient Golf Club of St. Andrews).

Originally St. Andrews offered twelve holes, which were not arranged so as to bring the golfers back to the clubhouse; on the contrary, they took them farther away. Also, because each tee was right next to a hole, the golfers actually had only eleven holes to play in one direction. At the end of eleven holes—since this left the players far from the clubhouse—it became customary for golfers to play the same eleven holes on the way back, for a total of twenty-two holes per round.

In 1764 St. Andrews decided that there wasn't enough distance between the first four holes and replaced them with just two holes, 400 or 500 yards apart. This meant that golfers now had only nine holes to play in each direction, for a total of eighteen holes in all. This number of holes seemed satisfactory, so it became the standard, with one significant modification.

Playing the same nine holes in two directions was awkward, involved long waits for other players, and—with balls flying in both directions—was downright dangerous. So the course at St. Andrews was changed to give golfers nine holes going away from the clubhouse and a different set of nine holes coming back. Since St. Andrews was a prestigious club and the one to be copied in those days, other clubs soon designed the same type of course and eighteen-hole courses became the standard.

Ever Wonder Why?

—oysters make pearls?

The type of oysters that make pearls spend most of their time on the sandy bottoms of tropical seas. When a grain of sand, or other foreign particle, gets inside of the oyster's shell and becomes an irritant, the oyster's system automatically begins coating the particle with a protective layer of nacre—mother-of-pearl. As layer after layer is added, the pearl is formed.

—you sometimes see a green tint on potato chips?

The green substance is chlorophyll that was produced when a part of the potato grew aboveground and was exposed to sunlight. This exposure also caused the production of another substance called solanine, which can be toxic.

—paratroopers yell "geronimo" when they jump out of the airplane?

It seems that, in the early days of the 82nd Airborne Division, paratroopers from Fort Benning, Georgia, went to a movie about the heroic exploits of the Apache Indian chief Geronimo. During their own exploits on the practice field, they began calling each other Geronimo and then shouting the name when they jumped from the plane.

—all of something referred to as "the whole nine yards"?

In this case the whole nine yards are the nine cubic yards of cement that certain rotating cement-mixer trucks can carry. If one wanted to take delivery of all the cement on the truck, he or she would ask for "the whole nine yards." Today the expression means all of anything.

Ever Wonder Why?

—sunsets are red?

When the sun is low on the horizon, its rays must pass through more of the earth's atmosphere to reach an observer. This means that the rays pass through more molecules and particles in the air that are capable of deflecting and scattering them. It is this scattering that causes a red sunset.

The sun's white light is actually a mixture of violet, blue, green, yellow, orange, and red light. When this light passes through the atmosphere, the light on the violet end of the spectrum is scattered much more easily than that on the red end. Therefore, by the time the light from a sun that is low on the horizon reaches an observer, all the colors except red have been scattered and filtered out.

—worms come out onto sidewalks after a rain?

Because their holes are full of water. They are simply moving to higher ground.

—something in the area of your specialty is "right down your alley"?

This was originally a baseball expression. In baseball an alley is one of several paths a ball can take into the outfield that makes the ball hard to catch. A player who feels that his or her specialty is hitting a ball down a particular one of these paths might promise to hit the next one "right down my alley." Eventually the expression was generalized to refer to any sort of specialty.

—the windows in textile mills are often painted over?

To keep the employees from looking out. In the days when textile mills were less computerized, a costly mistake could result if an employee became distracted while operating a piece of equipment such as a loom.

Ever Wonder Why?

—so many whales beach themselves?

Whales navigate using sound waves in much the same way as submarines do. They send out sound signals of a certain frequency and then measure how long it takes the signals to bounce off of the ocean floor and return. The longer it takes, the deeper the water. By this means whales are usually able to keep out of shallow water.

Sometimes, however—especially around shallow sandy bottoms—the whale's sound signals are partly absorbed by the sand and then bounced back and forth between the shallow bottom and the surface of the water. This delays the time it takes for the signal to get back to the whale, making the whale think that it is approaching deep water. The whale proceeds ahead and, to its surprise, finds itself beached in shallow water.

—sheriffs' badges are almost always star-shaped?

In primitive societies the star was believed to possess many magical powers, principal among which was the power to guard against danger and control evil forces. As recently as the Middle Ages the star was still considered by many to represent all-powerful forces. It is believed that because of its wide acceptance as the symbol of guardianship, the star was the natural choice as the symbol for the office of sheriff.

Ever Wonder Why?

—? is used to indicate a question?

At one time questions in Latin were indicated by following them with the word *questio*, the Latin word for question. This was obviously too cumbersome to work for very long, so it was soon abbreviated to "QO." But these letters were frequently mistaken for part of the last word in the question, so it was next decided to write them one over the other as ᢆ. This worked and was retained, but the ᢆ soon deteriorated to ᢆ then to ? and finally to ?

—a sudden fright sometimes cures hiccups?

Hiccups are spasms of the muscles in the diaphragm that are controlled by the vagus nerves. The spasms occur when the nerves are irritated, as by a full stomach, carbonated water, etc. It is sometimes possible to stop the spasms by giving the vagus nerves other tasks to perform. Since a sudden fright sends a flurry of signals down the vagus nerves to slow the heartbeat and lower blood pressure, this distraction often causes the nerves to forget about the spasms and the hiccups to stop.

—politicians sometimes give a visiting dignitary the "key to the city"?

This idea originated in the days when cities, or parts of cities, were protected by high walls and a gate. The gate, which was always locked at night, could be unlocked with a single key. When a gold version of this key was given to a visiting dignitary, it was a high honor since it symbolized the city's complete trust in him or her.

Ever Wonder Why?

—bats sleep upside down?

Since bats are nocturnal animals and must sleep during the daytime, it was natural for them to take up residence in dark recesses such as caves. And since they could not sleep on the floors of the caves without being attacked by predators, it was also natural that they find a way to sleep on or near the ceilings. Now if caves had been equipped with lots of shelflike platforms, it is likely that the bats would have learned to sleep upright on these in the same way birds sleep on limbs. But in the absence of such structures nature had to adapt bats to sleep the only way they could under these conditions—hanging upside down from the ceiling.

—we say "one fell swoop" to describe an act carried out swiftly?

In this expression the word *fell* has nothing to do with the verb "to fall" but comes instead from an Anglo-Saxon word, *fel*, meaning fierce or savage. This is the same *fel* found in the word *felon*. "One fell swoop," then, means "a sudden and fierce act," similar to the way a hawk swoops down suddenly and fiercely grabs its prey.

—you sometimes see large red or orange balls attached to high-tension power lines?

These balls are found in areas where there are low-flying aircraft, and they are put there to mark the wires so that such aircraft won't fly into them.

121

Ever Wonder Why?

—a horse's slow gallop is called a "canter"?

When pilgrims used to make their periodic treks on horseback to the shrine of Thomas à Becket at Canterbury, England, they typically rode along the old Kent road at a slow gait somewhere between a trot and a gallop. This gait, which was a bit peculiar to watch, became known as the Canterbury gallop. The term stuck and, over time, was gradually shortened until today that peculiar gait is called just a canter.

—eyes sometimes appear red in a flash photograph?

This occurs when a flash is so aimed that its light reflects off the back of the eye and into the camera lens. The red is caused by the blood vessels in the retinal tissue on the back of the eye.

—"in cahoots with" means in partnership with?

In parts of medieval Europe, at a time when there was little police protection, many bandits, robbers, and highwaymen ran rampant. Gangs of these criminals often stayed in makeshift cabins called "cahutes," and anyone thought to be in partnership with one of the gangs was described as being "in cahoots" (i.e., in cahutes) with them.

Ever Wonder Why?

—thirteen is called a baker's dozen?

At one time the problem of bakers' shortweighting their customers became so serious that laws were enacted imposing severe penalties for any baker caught doing this. This meant that bakers had to be very careful about the weight of the bread they sold. But in those days it was difficult to make bread loaves of uniform weight. So, to make absolutely sure that a dozen loaves sold to a shopkeeper didn't contain less than the required weight, the bakers often threw in a thirteenth loaf. These thirteen loaves became known as a baker's dozen. Later the term came to describe thirteen of anything.

—it is bad luck to walk under a ladder?

A ladder leaning against a wall forms a triangle, the symbol of the trinity and the mystic number three. It was once believed that to walk through the triangle would be to defy the trinity and become susceptible to the devil's ploys.

Ever Wonder Why?

—sidespin on a cue ball in the game of pool is called "English"?

Because it was invented by an Englishman.

Around 1825 an English billiards expert named Jack Carr began making seemingly impossible shots by putting a peculiar sideways twist on the cue ball. When other players inquired about the technique, Carr was able to convince them that the stroke could be performed only through the use of a special "twisting-chalk" that he was more than happy to sell them for half a crown. His business in magic twisting-chalk flourished until someone discovered that the twist could be put on the cue ball using any chalk at all. The Englishman's business quickly took a nosedive, but his special spin is still called "English" in remembrance of its inventor.

Index

126

127

128